UNITED STATES LEGAL DISCOURSE: LEGAL ENGLISH FOR FOREIGN LLMs

By

Craig Hoffman, J.D., Ph.D.
Georgetown University Law Center

Andrea Tyler, Ph.D.
Georgetown University, Department of Linguistics

AMERICAN CASEBOOK SERIES®

Mat #40353989

© 2008 Thomson/West
     610 Opperman Drive
     St. Paul, MN 55123
     1–800–313–9378

Printed in the United States of America

ISBN: 978–0–314–15994–6

 *TEXT IS PRINTED ON 10% POST CONSUMER RECYCLED PAPER*

Preface

We are very happy that you are taking this class. You will be learning about many related aspects of U.S. legal thinking and legal language, all of which will help you to more effectively use and evaluate U.S. Legal Discourse and begin to become a member of the U.S. Legal Discourse Community.

You have probably noticed that this textbook is shorter than your other textbooks. We have designed this textbook intentionally so that you will be spending much of your time reading and evaluating actual U.S. legal documents. Most of the documents that you will read will be in the Course Materials on your professor's TWEN site. Follow the instructions that are included with this textbook so that you can access these Course Materials.

In this class, you will be reading full-text documents. You have probably noticed that the documents in your other textbooks have been heavily edited. For example, if you are reading a typical law school textbook about U.S. Corporations, the textbook will be likely to have excerpts from several cases each of which focuses on a particular aspect of the law. The authors of the textbook delete information from the cases that is not directly relevant to the topics of the chapter in which the cases are contained. As a lawyer, you must learn to "edit" cases yourself. One of the goals of this course is to help you learn to do just that. In this class, you will learn how to approach many different types of legal documents so that you can become more proficient at getting the relevant information out of them. That is, you will learn to read efficiently.

In particular, you will be reading and evaluating three types of legal documents: 1) court cases, which are typically written by judges; 2) scholarly articles, which are typically written by legal academics; and 3) legal memorandums, which are typically written by lawyers. As you read these legal documents, you will be evaluating them on two levels. First, you will be reading them to learn about the law. That is, you will be using the documents to learn about the law so that you can address your client's legal question. Second, you will be reading them to learn about U.S. Legal Discourse. You will be evaluating the documents so that you can better understand the argumentation style and types of evidence that are most persuasive with U.S. lawyers. We will ask you to consider the choices U.S. legal writers make as they construct legal documents. In other words, you will be raising your awareness about the writer's role in U.S. Legal Discourse.

For example, when you look at court opinions, we will ask you to think about what the judge's purpose was in writing the opinion. That is, what is the exact legal question that the court is addressing and who is the audience for this document? Further, you will evaluate how the structure of the opinion reflects that purpose. Later, you will contrast this purpose and audience with those of the scholarly article and the legal memorandum. We will ask to consider how the writer's purpose varies in writing each of these documents. For instance, how does the legal scholar's purpose differ from that of the judge writing the court opinion? Finally, how do the writers' different purposes reflect the different roles that the documents have in U.S. Legal Discourse?

As you become familiar with analyzing legal documents in this way, you will more deeply understand how they (and their writers) contribute to a complete analysis of your client's legal problem. This type of close reading of texts will help you to get more out of all of your reading. You will simultaneously be learning about the law, learning about how U.S. lawyers think about the law, and improving your control of U.S. Legal Discourse.

Using the TWEN site is integral to this class in general and to using this book in particular. Before beginning your reading for this class, be sure that you have done all of the following things:

1) You have registered your Westlaw password;

2) You have logged on to TWEN;

3) You have registered for your professor's TWEN site;

4) You have opened your professor's TWEN site; and

5) You have clicked on the tab for Course Materials.

If you have trouble doing any of these things, please contact Westlaw or ask your law librarian for assistance. You could also ask one of your classmates to help you. It is important that you begin talking with your classmates as soon as possible. You will learn a great deal by talking with your classmates, and talking with your classmates is a major part of this class. Perhaps a short discussion about your preparations for this class could begin a friendship that will last forever.

Welcome to the United States Legal Discourse Community.

Table of Contents

———

UNITED STATES LEGAL DISCOURSE: LEGAL ENGLISH FOR FOREIGN LLMs

*

Chapter 1

BECOMING FLUENT IN UNITED STATES LEGAL DISCOURSE

1.1 INTRODUCTION

When most non-native English speakers think about U.S. legal writing, they think about Legal English. To these students, Legal English often means vocabulary and grammar. Somehow, students have been led to believe that memorizing legal terms and practicing grammar rules will make them better and more knowledgeable U.S. legal writers and, consequently, better and more knowledgeable U.S. lawyers.

When most native English speakers think about U.S. legal writing, they too tend to think about Legal English. To these students, Legal English often also means vocabulary and grammar. Native English speakers who are new to the law also seem to believe that memorizing legal terms and complicated legal phrases will make them better and more knowledgeable legal writers and, consequently, better and more knowledgeable lawyers.

When legal linguists[1] think about U.S. legal writing, they think about Legal Discourse. To a legal linguist, individual words or individual sentences cannot be interpreted without understanding the contexts in which they are used. As we proceed through this book, we will be introducing you to different types of legal texts. We will be analyzing these texts not for their vocabulary and grammar, but for how they contribute to U.S. Legal Discourse. We do not argue that knowing legal vocabulary and English grammar is unimportant. Rather, we argue that vocabulary and grammar are only a small part of what LL.M. students need to know to be successful in U.S. law school.

We admit that, at least sometimes, it is simple vocabulary that distinguishes English from Legal English. For example, the sentence in (1) can have (at least) two meanings in English.

---

1. A legal linguist is anyone who is trained in discourse analysis and the law. By the end of this semester, you too will become well-informed legal linguists.

1

(1) John gave Mary no consideration.

In a non-legal context, Sentence (1) could mean that John ignored Mary or that he did not, in some relevant way, consider her qualifications—for example, for a job. It would mean something like Sentence (2).

(2) John did not consider Mary.

In a legal context, Sentence (1) could mean something entirely different. Depending on the context, it could have one of the "plain English meanings" described above. If, however, John and Mary were involved in a contract dispute, John might argue that a contract does not exist between them because John had given nothing of value to Mary— that is, he gave Mary no legal consideration.[2] In fact, Sentence (1) is the most precise way to convey this meaning. Sentence (2) is likely not to "mean" the same as Sentence (1) in Legal Discourse.

In some cases, then, the difference between English and Legal English appears to be as simple as knowing the particular definition of "consideration." Given just this type of example, you might agree with those who say mastering Legal Discourse is no more than learning a few specialized terms.

1.2 LEGAL ENGLISH VS. LEGAL DISCOURSE

Beyond the definitions of individual words, Legal Discourse is characterized by a certain type of argumentation. In this class, we will refer to this as Common Law Argumentation. In the next Chapter, we will explore common law argumentation in more detail. At this point, we would like you to simply recognize some of the ways in which Common Law Argumentation differs from forms of argumentation that you might be used to. We would also like to point out how important Common Law Argumentation is to U.S. Legal Discourse and contrast it to what is commonly understood to be Legal English.

As an introduction to this new way of looking at argumentation, let us consider a simple example of how a U.S. lawyer might address a client's legal problem. First, the U.S. lawyer would gather the facts of his case. He would then collect the relevant legal sources, and, finally, he would write his analysis of how the law would most likely apply to the specific facts of his client's case. We will assume that the lawyer doing the analysis is a beginning LL.M. student who was not trained in a common law system. We will first evaluate his analysis as a matter of Legal English. We will then evaluate his analysis as a matter of U.S. Legal Discourse.

---

2. If you are simply unable to understand a specific legal term, such as "consideration," you could use a legal dictionary such as Blacks Law Dictionary to find a definition. The dictionary, however, cannot explain to you other relevant aspects of English grammar or the effect of a specific legal context on the interpretation of an actual sentence. For a discussion of the limits of using dictionaries for interpreting Legal Discourse, see Craig Hoffman, *Curbing the Urge to Resort to the Dictionary When Interpreting Legal Texts*, 6 N.Y.U. J. Legis. & Pub. Pol'y, 401 (2002–2003).

To begin, consider the following facts:

You are an Associate at a U.S. law firm. Assume that your firm's client is a public official accused of accepting a bribe. A government agent, posing as a corrupt lobbyist for a pharmaceutical company, offered your client $1 million in a conversation regarding the upcoming vote on a bill that would favor the pharmaceutical industry. Your client accepted the $1 million. Your client has been charged under the relevant bribery statute. As a defense to the charge of bribery under the statute, however, your client contends that he had planned all along to vote in favor of the legislation. Therefore, he was not actually "bribed." The money was simply a gift. Assume further that a Partner at your firm has asked you to write a memorandum evaluating whether a court would be likely to accept the client's proposed defense.

The relevant statutory law is the New Columbia bribery statute in (3).

(3) New Columbia[3] Statute: Receiving a Bribe

(a) A public servant commits the crime of receiving a bribe if the public servant

> (1) solicits a benefit with the intent that the public servant's vote, opinion, judgment, action, decision, or exercise of discretion as a public servant will be influenced; or

> (2) accepts or agrees to accept a benefit upon an agreement or understanding that the public servant's vote, opinion, judgment, action, decision, or exercise of discretion as a public servant will be influenced.

(b) Receiving a bribe is a class B felony.

Having read the statute and some other legal sources, the LL.M. student writes a short memorandum, which includes the following paragraph in (4):

> (4) Section 11.56.110 of the New Columbia bribery statute **calls it a crime** for a public official to agree to "accept a benefit upon an agreement or understanding that the public servant's vote ... will be influenced." Scholars who have recently written about this **code** agree that the government **should prove** that the public official actually changed his vote in response to the offer of a benefit. For example, Professor John Smith of Georgetown University Law Center, who is the world authority on "crimes of language" has analyzed the development of U.S. bribery law. He has determined that **"a benefit that is offered after the public official has made up his mind about an issue cannot be considered to be a bribe. Bribery requires a specific *quid pro quo*."** Because our

---

3. For this set of examples, we refer to "New Columbia" rather than to an actual U.S. state. All states have their own bribery statutes and case law interpreting those statutes. The point of these examples is to demonstrate discourse features of legal texts; it is not intended to be lesson about any state's bribery laws. Assume that New Columbia has a statutory code and a court system that includes New Columbia Trial Courts, New Columbia Appellate Courts, and a New Columbia Supreme Court.

client did not change his vote in response to the benefit offered, he **will not be guilty** of bribery under the statute.

In order to become a fluent user of Legal Discourse, it is important that you be able to criticize legal texts. Let us criticize the paragraph in (4), first, as a matter of Legal English. In many ways, this short paragraph might seem perfectly adequate. Nevertheless, some of the phrasing in the paragraph would not seem "correct" to native speakers of English. I have highlighted some of the phrases that signal that this paragraph may not have been written by a native English speaker familiar with U.S. Legal English. One way to criticize this paragraph would be to point out the "mistakes" of Legal English.

For example, the phrase "calls it a crime" is not correct usage as a matter of Legal English. Lawyers refer to criminal statutes as "making" certain acts a crime, rather than "calling" those acts a crime. Also, when U.S. lawyers refer to a specific code section, they say "statute" and not "code." The word code usually refers to an entire body of related statutory law; for example, the Criminal Code of New Columbia. Each code provisions is referred to as a statute. Notice, too, that the quote attributed to Professor Smith is not cited; that is, the writer has not told the reader where he could find the quoted language. We will see later that citation is extremely important tin U.S. Legal Discourse.

Further, the phrases "should prove" and "will not be guilty" represent improper uses of modal verbs. When discussing what a state has to show to prove that someone has committed a crime, lawyers would use the modal "must." This indicates that if the state does not prove this, it will lose the case. The modal "should" is too soft here. In the next example, a lawyer would probably not use the verb phrase, "will not be guilty" in this context. The lawyer here is trying to predict what a court would do in our case. A lawyer can never be 100 percent sure of what a court would do. In this case, the lawyer would probably say "it is unlikely that a court would..." Because a court's ruling could depend on many other factors, the lawyer would "hedge" a bit on the conclusion.

The changes that we have suggested for this paragraph fall under the categories of Legal English. Making the suggested changes, the paragraph, now in (5), appears to be "better."

(5) Section 11.56.110 of the New Columbia bribery statute **makes it a crime** for a public official to agree to "accept a benefit upon an agreement or understanding that the public servant's vote ... will be influenced." Scholars who have recently written about this **statute** agree that the government **must prove** that the public official actually changed his vote in response to the offer of a benefit. For example, Professor John Smith of Georgetown University Law Center, who is the world authority on bribery law, has analyzed the development of U.S. bribery law. He has determined that "a benefit that is offered after the public official has made up his mind about an issue cannot be considered to be a bribe. Bribery requires a

specific *quid pro quo*."[4] Because our client did not change his vote in response to the benefit offered, **a court is unlikely to find our client guilty** of bribery under the statute.

The Legal English analysis that we just considered focuses on the sentence-level and word-level aspects of the text in (4). We "corrected" the words and phrases that appeared to be "errors" of Legal English. As we begin to look more closely at U.S. Legal Discourse, however, we will begin to focus on a somewhat "higher" level of analysis of legal texts. Let us now focus on the discourse-level aspects of the text in (4).

U.S. lawyers read U.S legal texts looking for very specific types of information. For example, when a U.S. lawyer reads a paragraph like (4), he is interested not only in the writer's legal conclusion, but he is also interested in a very specific type of legal reasoning—that is, he is keenly interested in how the writer analyzed prior law in coming to his conclusion. For example, if the writer has not adequately analyzed prior case law where courts have discussed the application of this statute to other facts, the reader will not accept the writer's discussion as adequate as a matter of proper U.S. Legal Discourse. In fact, the writer's primary job in composing any legal text is to fulfill the reader's expectations about the Legal Discourse.

Let us look critically at the paragraph in (5). First, notice that the writer provides some very useful information to the reader. It identifies and quotes the relevant statute; it refers to an authority that precisely addresses the issue in the case; and it makes a specific conclusion about the client's situation. To someone not familiar with U.S. Legal Discourse, this might seem to be a nice example of proper legal analysis. To a U.S. lawyer, however, this memorandum is virtually worthless. Even though the grammar and syntax in the memorandum are perfect, and no word is used in a way that is inconsistent with Legal Discourse, other features of the analysis render it immediately recognizable as non-U.S. legal reasoning. Even though some of the Legal English errors have been corrected, the paragraph in (5) would not be considered adequate to a U.S. lawyer. Although the paragraph fulfills some of the reader's expectations, it lacks important discourse features. Compare the paragraph in (5) to the one in (6).

(6) It is unlikely that our client will be found guilty of receiving a bribe under New Columbia law. 11 New Columbia Statutes 11.56.110 (2003). The statute requires the accused to have accepted a benefit "upon agreement or understanding that the public servant's vote ... will be influenced."[5] The New Columbia Supreme

---

4. John Smith. The Law of Bribery. Georgetown University Press (2005).

5. New Columbia Statute: Receiving a Bribe

a) A public servant commits the crime of receiving a bribe if the public servant

(1) solicits a benefit with the intent that the public servant's vote, opinion, judgment, action, decision, or exercise of discretion as a public servant will be influenced; or

(2) accepts or agrees to accept a benefit upon an agreement or understanding that the public servant's vote, opinion,

Court has recently ruled that a public official who has already made up his mind about a vote cannot "be influenced" to vote the same way. *State v. Jones*, 232 New Columbia Reporter 364 (2005). In *State v. Jones*, the court considered a public official who had made several statements to the press that he was determined to vote in favor of specific legislation that benefited the tobacco industry. The state later prosecuted him for accepting lavish presents, including sports cars and exotic vacations, from representatives of a major tobacco company. The court concluded that this activity did not constitute a "bribe" under the statute.

In *State v. Brown*, however, the New Columbia Court of Appeals ruled that a public official who changed his vote after receiving a benefit from a lobbyist had "received a bribe" under New Columbia 11.56.110. *State v. Brown*, 229 New Columbia Appeals Reporter 782 (2006). Our client seems to be in the same position as the defendant in *State v. Jones*. Because our client did intend to vote in favor of the pharmaceutical bill before the benefit was offered to him, it is unlikely that a New Columbia court will find him guilty of receiving a bribe.

The New Columbia Supreme Court has also ruled that it is the burden of the state to show that the public official changed his vote in response to the benefit offered. *State v. White*, 214 New Columbia Reporter 23 (2001). Because the defendant in *State v. Jones* had made public statements prior to the alleged bribe, it was difficult for the government to meet its burden to show that the defendant had changed his vote because of the benefit offered. Although no evidence of prior statements exists in our case, it is the government that must prove that our client changed his vote in response to the promise of the benefit. *See State v. Black*, 223 New Columbia Reporter 859 (2002) (holding that the government bears a high burden of proving a causal relationship between a vote by a public official and the promise of a benefit).

As you can see, the writer of the paragraphs in (6) has taken quite a different approach from the writer of the paragraph in (5). As we will discuss in Chapter 2, the writer of the paragraphs in (6) is using a form of argument that his U.S. legal audience is expecting. Notice how the writer identifies prior case law that has addressed similar issues. The writer also compares the facts of those other cases to the facts of the case under discussion. On each of the issues that he discussed, the writer makes conclusions about the new case based on his analysis of the prior cases. In U.S. Legal Discourse, we call this type of reasoning Common Law Argumentation. In later Chapters of this book, we will explore this type of argumentation in greater detail. For now, it is important only that you recognize the different approaches that the writers in (5) and

judgment, action, decision, or exercise of discretion as a public servant will be influenced.

(3) Receiving a bribe is a class B felony.

(6) have taken. A U.S. lawyer, who understands how the U.S. federal common law legal system works, is always interested in seeing how prior relevant courts have decided a legal issue. As you become more familiar with the U.S. common law legal system, you will become more familiar with the discourse expectations of the U.S. legal audience. In fact, arguments such as those in (5) will seem "ungrammatical" to you as a matter of U.S. Legal Discourse.

As you can see, evaluating a legal text according to the discourse expectations of the reader involves more than simply focusing on word choice and grammar. To fully understand U.S. Legal Discourse, you must understand how lawyers evaluate and use texts in their Discourse Community. A Discourse Community develops social and intellectual norms and expectations. All members of the Discourse Community share these norms and expectations. Becoming an "insider" or member of the U.S. Legal Discourse Community goes beyond being able to recognize certain vocabulary and phrases are commonly used in the community's texts. More important, you must fully understand these other factors— the discourse factors—that characterize how the U.S. Legal Discourse Community uses legal texts.

In this class, you will learn to evaluate several types of legal texts as you participate in the representation of a client. Although you will certainly improve your mastery of Legal English as you proceed through this semester, you will also improve your mastery and awareness of Legal Discourse.

1.3 CLOSE READING EXERCISE 1: AN OPINION OF THE U.S. SUPREME COURT

The authors of this text are Legal Linguists. We have analyzed legal texts and studied not only how these texts work as individual documents but also how they contribute to a larger Legal Discourse. As we proceed through this course, we will introduce you to various types of legal texts. For each text, we will explore how it functions in U.S. Legal Discourse. To begin this process, you will now read an important U.S. Supreme Court opinion, *Erie R.R. Co. v. Tompkins*,[6] which was written by an extremely well-respected U.S. Supreme Court Justice, Louis Brandeis. By reading this opinion, you will deepen your understanding about U.S. Legal Discourse in two ways. First, you will learn more about the U.S. legal system. Second, you will learn more about what types of legal arguments are acceptable to the U.S. legal audience.

All U.S. lawyers share an understanding of how our federal, common law legal system works. That is, the structure of our legal system and the interrelationship of the federal and state court systems are part of the "background knowledge" of all U.S. lawyers. As members of the U.S. Legal Discourse Community, U.S. lawyers speak and write about the law based on this shared understanding of our legal system. It is very important for LL.M. students to learn as much about possible about

---

6. Erie v. Tompkins, 304 U.S. 64 (1938).

how the U.S. legal system works so that they can begin to share this important background knowledge with their U.S. colleagues.

In the *Erie* opinion, Justice Brandeis writes a majority decision that directs federal courts to apply state law when they are ruling on state law matters. In order to understand this ruling, you have to understand a few things about the interrelationship between the federal courts and the state courts. As you read this opinion, try to infer from the discussion what background knowledge about the U.S. legal system Justice Brandeis is assuming his readers will have. For example, under what conditions can a federal court decide a case that only involves state law? Why might a plaintiff decide to file such a suit in federal court rather than state court? When deciding such cases, how do the federal courts decide what the proper analysis of the state law should be? All of these issues are discussed in the context of the *Erie* case.

In addition to reading critically to learn more about the U.S. legal system itself, you can also learn more about U.S. legal argumentation. In *Erie*, the U.S. Supreme Court is faced with a difficult question. The Court ultimately writes an opinion that overrules a line of earlier cases that it now believes had misinterpreted a federal statute. As members of the U.S. Legal Discourse Community, U.S. lawyers all understand that this is an extraordinary event. Because of our strong adherence to precedent, courts are quite reluctant to overrule prior cases. In most instances, courts will try to reach decisions that are, in some sense, predictable by analyzing prior case law. In our common law system, the process of deciding new cases is based on the judge's analysis of prior cases. Because members of the U.S. Legal Discourse Community expect that judges will decide cases by analogy to prior cases, court opinions that provide careful analysis of prior cases are highly valued. Because it is quite rare for the U.S. Supreme Court to overrule its prior decisions, Justice Brandeis is quite careful to support his decision with sound common law reasoning.

As you read Justice Brandeis's opinion in *Erie*, notice how he makes his legal arguments. Pay attention to what sorts of legal sources he relies on in supporting his arguments. Reading the opinion this way will help you to understand what sorts of arguments are appealing to U.S. lawyers. In doing this type of critical reading, you are reading to learn about how arguments are made in U.S. Legal Discourse. That is a different task from reading to learn information about a particular area of the law. Reading critically will help you to become more comfortable with U.S. Legal Discourse.

Again, as you read this opinion, please focus two things: first, try to focus on the exact legal question that Justice Brandeis is addressing and what that question assumes about the interrelationship between the federal and state courts; next, pay careful attention to the structure of the legal arguments that Justice Brandeis makes. Please read not only Justice Brandeis's majority opinion, but also read the dissenting opinion by Justice Butler and the concurring opinion by Justice McReynolds and

Justice Reed (concurring in part). This opinion appears as one of the first items in the COURSE MATERIALS section of your TWEN site. To see the opinion, click on the item that says "Chapter 1: *Erie v. Tompkins*" in COURSE MATERIALS. Next, click the link that says "304 U.S. 64." Also on your TWEN site, you will find the text of the federal statute that the Court is discussing ("Chapter 1: 28 U.S.C.A. 1652") and the text of Article III of the United States Constitution, which sets out the jurisdiction of the federal courts ("Chapter 1: United States Constitution, Article III"). Please read *Erie v. Tompkins* as well as the statute and Article III before you come to our next class.

Chapter 2

DISCOURSE PRACTICES
IN REPRESENTING
A CLIENT

2.1 INTRODUCTION

In this class, you will learn about United States Legal Discourse by carefully and critically reading primary and secondary legal resources. Through the tasks of criticizing and creating legal texts, you will begin to better understand the U.S. legal audience, and you will become better prepared to interact with U.S. lawyers. One of the most important things that you can learn while attending law school in the United States is how U.S. lawyers use case law to analyze legal problems. We will be focusing on a specific client with a specific legal problem. By addressing your client's legal problem and criticizing the relevant legal sources, you will begin to see how a U.S. lawyer would analyze a complex legal problem. In addition, you will also learn more about the U.S. legal system.

One of the most interesting aspects of the U.S. legal system is the interrelationship of the state and federal courts. For example, as you will see, a lawyer might file a lawsuit in a New York state court on a matter of New York state law. She could, however, file the same lawsuit in federal court, if, for example, the parties are from different states. If she were to file the suit in federal court, the federal court would probably apply New York state law in deciding the case. As you have seen in the *Erie v. Tompkins* opinion, this interrelationship of the state and federal courts and the procedural and substantive laws that they apply is sometimes quite complex, but it reflects the most fundamental aspects of our federal constitutional system of government. Fully exploring all of the fascinating issues that arise in this context is the subject of several other law school classes—it could, in fact, consume an entire academic career. Our goal here is to simply introduce you to one example of how this interrelationship plays a part in a client's specific legal problem. Having carefully examined this client's problem, you will be aware of some of the important questions to ask when you approach similar legal problems—either in your other classes or in your own legal practice when you complete your LL.M.

You will also begin to recognize good examples of common law legal argumentation. When judges in the United States decide cases, they are trying to integrate the facts of the case they are deciding into the existing common law. Judges usually refer to the reasoning that other judges have used in prior cases when deciding their own cases. As you will see, some cases are mandatory (or binding) authority on a particular judge, and others are more or less persuasive authority. For example, in the federal court system, opinions of the United States Supreme Court are mandatory authority on all lower federal courts and on all state courts when those courts are deciding federal issues. Opinions of the Federal Court of Appeals for the First Circuit are mandatory authority on all Federal District Courts and all state courts deciding federal issues within the First Circuit, but they are only persuasive authority in all other circuits.

One of the most interesting challenges for lawyers in the United States is to evaluate the persuasiveness of authority that exists on a certain legal subject. As you learn to evaluate and criticize the legal documents in this book, you will begin to understand how U.S. lawyers create common law arguments based on mandatory and persuasive legal authority.

2.2   DISCOURSE PRACTICES IN A U.S. LAW FIRM

We will be analyzing a client's legal problem as if we were a U.S. law firm. After being introduced to the client's legal problem in an Initial Meeting, we will examine the types of legal sources that a U.S. lawyer would use to address the client's legal problem. Ultimately, we will analyze an example of a legal memorandum that a U.S. lawyer might write in which he would evaluate the relevant legal sources and make a prediction about how a court might treat his client's legal problem. By analyzing the client's problem and examining how a U.S. lawyer is likely to approach it, you will learn more about U.S. Legal Discourse practices, and you will become a participant in U.S. Legal Discourse.

We will situate our problem in the U.S. law office. We will focus on the private law firm. Most, if not all, of what we say here about the discourse in the law firm will apply equally to other legal situations— government law offices; small practice firms; public interest and not-for-profit law offices. It is customary in all of these settings for lawyers to talk with each other about their clients' legal problems. As you become familiar with your client's problem, and as you begin to evaluate the legal sources relevant to addressing this problem, you will begin to understand how U.S. lawyers think about practicing law.

Before we introduce you to your client, we would like to explain a little more about the setting in which the representation takes place. In addition, we would like to introduce you to some of the background legal concepts that will help you to evaluate your client's legal situation. First, we will tell you a little bit about the social system in which your representation will occur; we refer to this as the U.S. Law Firm Discourse. In many ways, it will be similar to the way law firms work in your country. We will also introduce you to the reasoning that U.S. lawyers use in making arguments about a client's legal problem. We call this Common Law Argumentation. U.S. lawyers use Common Law Argumentation in all aspects of U.S. Legal Discourse. At the end of this Chapter, we will ask you to read a U.S. law review article. As you read the article, you will be paying attention to not only the substantive law being discussed but also the Common Law Argumentation that the authors use to support their legal conclusions. Finally, we will give you a brief introduction to U.S. legal citation. Legal citation gives valuable information to legal readers, and it is an important part of Legal Discourse. As you become a more experienced user (and critic) of U.S. legal texts, you will become a more comfortable participant in U.S. Legal Discourse.

2.3   UNDERSTANDING LAW FIRM DISCOURSE

Welcome to U.S. Law Firm Discourse. There are many participants in this discourse: lawyers, clients, judges, scholars, and all of the various texts that they write. All of these actors and texts are parts of a complex discourse that you will learn about. Let us first explore the workings of our law firm. We will refer to our law office as the USLD Law Firm. Our USLD Law Firm has the structure of most large U.S. law firms. Several lawyers, each of whom have been practicing law for many years, are partners in the firm. The Partners do most of the interacting with clients. They speak to the clients; they exchange letters and e-mails with the clients; they play golf with the clients. Because most law firms are organized as partnerships, the senior attorneys are Partners of the firm. They share all of the profits of the firm in accordance with their respective partnership shares. For example, if Sally Smith has a 10 percent partnership interest in the firm, she will receive 10 percent of the net profits of the firm at the end of the year. While the Partners of the firm are chatting with clients and playing golf, someone has to do the legal work of research and writing. Those attorneys are employees of the law firm partnership; they are called Associates. Associates are less experienced lawyers (usually between one and ten years out of law school) and the firm bills clients much less for their time than it does for the Partners' time. In our USLD Law Firm, you will assume the role of the Associate lawyer.

Throughout this book, we will be referring to Legal Discourse, Law Firm Discourse or just Discourse. U.S. Law Firm Discourse is a sub-set of all U.S. Legal Discourse. For example, all of the conversations that you have with other attorneys are part of this Discourse; all of the cases that you will read are part of this Discourse. It is important for you to understand the complexity and the organization of all of the components of this Discourse. As you progress through this class, not only will you become more familiar with the English language, but also you will become more familiar with United States Legal Discourse

2.4   THE DISCOURSE OF THE INITIAL MEETING

In the beginning phase of the Discourse, it is common for the Associate to meet with the Partner, either in the Partner's office or in a conference room at the firm. At this meeting, the Partner generally explains the facts of the case to the Associate. Good Associates always carry a legal pad with them when they attend these meetings with Partners. Partners like to see Associates write notes during these meetings. Partners like this for many reasons. First, after the meeting, the Partner will assume that the Associate remembers all of the facts of the case. In fact, the Partner will rely on the Associate to both remember everything that happens in this Initial Meeting and everything that happens in the case after the meeting. It is considered very bad form for the Associate to appear at the meeting without a legal pad (or a laptop computer).

When the Associate leaves the Initial Meeting, she returns to her office and creates a document to which she and the Partner may refer later if either of them has any questions about the facts of the case; we will refer to the text as the Client Intake Memo. In fact, the Associate often will add to the Client Intake Memo throughout the Discourse as new facts emerge or old facts change. It is very important that the Associate is clear about the facts of the case, and the Associate is encouraged to ask questions during and after the meeting if she is unclear about anything that the Partner or the client said. The purpose of the Client Intake Memo, therefore, is to keep an objective catalog of the facts in the case. The intended audience for this text is the Partner who assigned it and any attorney in the law firm who might at some point be involved in the case. In some sense, the Associate herself is a member of the intended audience for this text. The function of this text is to provide all members of the discourse (that is, the representation of this client) a comprehensive narrative about the facts of this case.

We will ask you to prepare a Client Intake Memo after you have been introduced to our client. In order to prepare this Client Intake Memo, you must be aware of the function that this text will serve in the Discourse of your representation of the client. In other words, you have to understand the purpose of the Client Intake Memo and what its intended audience will use it for. In fact, as we evaluate different legal texts in this class, you should always try to determine who the author is, why he is writing this particular text, and what legal audience he is writing it for. Asking yourselves these questions will help you both to better understand U.S. Legal Discourse and to become a more active participant in it.

Instead of inviting the Associate to the client meeting, in many ways, it might be easier for the Partner to simply sit down and write a description of the facts of the case and just give it to the Associate. This rarely happens. This discourse practice of Associates' learning about the facts of a case orally has some practical advantages. First, if the Associate knows that she must listen carefully enough to be able to draft a Client Intake Memo, she is likely to take very good notes during the Initial Meeting. In fact, writing reinforces thought in ways that listening does not. The act of taking careful notes is the first step to serious thinking about a topic. It is always important for writers to put information into their own words. The act of paraphrasing forces the writer to make decisions about what information is important. Taking good notes is important both in the classroom and in the law office. Further, the task of writing the Client Intake Memo reinforces the Associate's understanding of the facts of the client's case. It helps the Associate to begin to think about the legal issues she will research. These two steps in the Associate's thinking process are gone if the Partner simply hands the Associate a written assignment.

In addition, the Partner may use the discourse situation of the Initial Meeting to think about the client's problem. Sometimes, the Partner will not have completely thought about the client's problem before the Initial Meeting. As the Partner talks with the Associate, he might discover issues he had not considered before. The Initial Meeting is both a time for conveying information and, perhaps, strengthening the understanding of both the Partner and the Associate. There is also an economic factor. Partners bill clients at much higher hourly rates than Associates. Because preparing a Client Intake Memo takes more time than the Initial Meeting, it is more economical for the Associate to do the writing. This discourse practice of the Initial Meeting allocates costs efficiently; it gives the Associate, who is less familiar with the case, the opportunity to spend time on thinking and writing and gives the Partner, who are more familiar with the case, the opportunity to spend more time finding new clients and playing golf.

2.5 PREPARING FOR THE INITIAL MEETING: BACKGROUND READING

In many cases, an Associate will have had some experience in a particular topic of law. In U.S. firms, Associates sometimes specialize in certain areas of the law. For example, a bankruptcy specialist would be expected to know the major parts of federal bankruptcy legislation, some of the major cases in the area, and, perhaps, some of the scholarly literature in the area. In other cases, younger Associates might have no familiarity at all with the legal area that the client's case involves. When this happens, a Partner will often give the Associate some background reading to do before the Initial Meeting. If the Associate does some background reading, it is more likely that she will be able to absorb the information she hears in the Initial Meeting. Generally, when people hear information, they make associations with other information that they already have. People are more likely to remember information if they can relate it to other "frames" of information that they have developed.

2.6 DISCOURSE PRACTICE 1: READ THE ASSIGN-MENT EMAIL

Go to your TWEN site and click the button marked COURSE MATERIALS. Find the item in the list of COURSE MATERIALS called "Chapter 2: Email from the Partner about the Urbania Case." Click on that item. Before you continue reading here, please read the e-mail.

Practices differ among Partners and among law firms. Sometimes communications such as this will take place by phone. Other times, a Partner might go to the Associate's office and verbally invite the Associate to the meeting and hand the Associate a copy or citation to the article. Most of these communications in law offices are done by e-mail.

Although it is deceptively short, this e-mail from the Partner contains a good deal of valuable information. For example, the Partner has indicated that the client is the sovereign, Urbania, and the meeting will have something to do with restructuring a bond issue (whatever that means). The email also tells the Associate that she must "get up to speed" on the topic of sovereign bonds. This English idiom means that the Associate should learn as much about the restructuring of sovereign bonds as soon as possible. The Partner has suggested that you "get up to speed" by reading a law review article.

2.7 WHAT IS A LAW REVIEW ARTICLE?

As you read the article, you should be aware of a few things about the document and its content. You should also think about the authors' purpose in writing the article and who its intended audience is. In general, law professors contribute most of the scholarly articles to U.S. Legal Discourse. Practicing lawyers may write short articles for various professional journals; however, law faculty members contribute the bulk of the scholarly articles. The most common place for them to publish their work is in law reviews, which are journals that are published by U.S. law schools. Most U.S. law schools have one main journal: for example, The Georgetown Law Journal is the main journal for Georgetown University Law Center. In addition to the main journal, law schools have several other specialized journals, which publish articles on specific areas of the law. Georgetown University has several law reviews. Each of these journals is managed by a board of student editors. The student editors read manuscripts that faculty members and students send to them, and they choose the articles that they want to publish.

Law review articles are what we call secondary sources. They are not part of the law, but they can be a valuable resource for you to begin your research on a topic of law about which you know very little. It is always helpful to see how a knowledgeable writer has addressed legal questions similar to yours. Remember, however, that the writers are not impartial judges. As all authors, they are writers with a point of view. Although their ideas may be compelling, they are not in any sense legally binding. Scholarly articles, therefore, are not commonly referenced in legal briefs to a court.

2.8 RECOGNIZING COMMON LAW ARGUMENTA-TION

Before we take a close look at the law review article, it is important for you to begin to become familiar with the distinctive form of argumentation found in U.S. Legal Discourse, Common Law Argumentation. You have heard about the differences between civil law and common law legal systems and could no doubt offer solid definitions of the two. However, understanding the differences in how arguments are constructed in the two discourses is a more complicated matter. Learning how to recognize Common Law Argumentation in U.S. Legal Discourse and produce it in your own writing is a central challenge for effectively navigating U.S. law school and communicating with U.S. lawyers.

All good legal arguments begin with a clear articulation of the facts of the case at hand and identification of the pertinent legal issues the case raises. This is true for both common law discourse and civil law discourse. Many of the initial points in U.S. Legal Discourse will feel familiar. However, once the facts and issues are laid out, the argumentation begins to look rather different.

As you read U.S. legal cases, law review articles, and memorandums produced by U.S. lawyers, you will observe that they refer extensively to prior legal cases. Of course, they also refer to pertinent statutes, but far less so than in civil law discourse because in a common law system prior cases form a fundamental part of the law itself. Although judges in the U.S. system have more power to extend the law than judges in a civil law system, they are, nevertheless, strictly limited by precedent. Judges are not at liberty to make up whatever new law they want as they examine the facts of a case before them and determine the outcome. They are obligated to consider how the facts and issues of the case at hand compare to previous cases involving the same issues. This includes paying close attention to the reasoning the judges used as they decided the previous cases. One of the unique aspects of a common law system is that the judge's rationale for applying law in a particular way to the particular set of facts in the case at hand is as much a part of the law as the actual ruling. One important responsibility that every judge has in writing a legal opinion is to demonstrate how the thinking involved in his decision is linked to and grows out of previous legal decisions.

2.8.1 The Common Law Rubric

As U.S. lawyers and judges discuss prior cases and how they relate to the case at hand, their arguments usually include four basic components. Recognizing these components will help you to understand how U.S. lawyers construct and conceptualize legal arguments. We will refer to these components as the Common Law (CL) Rubric. A "rubric" is a set of criteria that members of a discourse use to evaluate the effectiveness of a text. As a rubric, it is meant as a guide, not a rigid template that must always be mechanically followed. The CL Rubric has the following components, which serve as criteria for evaluating the effectiveness of arguments in U.S. Legal Discourse. We will be referring to these components as Steps in a legal argument.

The Common Law (CL) Rubric

> Step 1: identifying a legally significant prior case and the key, legally significant facts of that case [what is significant is, of course, determined by the particular issues raised by the client's case];
>
> Step 2: explaining the rationale the court used in deciding the case;
>
> Step 3: explaining how the facts in the prior cases are either similar to or different from the facts of their client's case; and
>
> Step 4: drawing on the reasoning the court used in the prior case, in combination with the similarities or differences between the two cases, a prediction of how the court *is likely* to rule on the client's case.

Not all examples of Common Law Argumentation will contain exactly these four steps. For instance, in a legal opinion (a court case), you will not find Step 4. The judge does not predict how she is likely to rule on the case; she simply provides the court's ruling. In a legal memorandum written by an Associate on a particular point of law, however, Step 4 is crucial; the Associate must, once she has researched all the pertinent law, inform the Partner how she thinks the court *might* decide the client's case. Also, the four steps will not necessarily appear in this order. Often the writer will intertwine two steps in a single sentence. Sometimes the lawyer or judge may feel that the precedent is clearly enough established that she does not need to give a full account of the significant facts of the prior case and will feel that simply mentioning the case and the judge's reasoning is sufficient. However, as someone new to U.S. Legal Discourse, you will find it useful to keep these four steps of Common Law Argumentation in mind as you read cases, journal articles, and memos and as you write your own Legal Discourse for an audience of U.S. lawyers.

2.8.2 Recognizing the CL Rubric in a Sample Legal Discourse

Now let's consider some examples of Common Law Argumentation. The following examples address certain specific aspects of a particular legal case. This is the only time that we will be addressing these particular issues in this book; however, looking at these simple examples should help you to become familiar with the kind of Common Law Argumentation that you will see in the more complex examples that will be involved in your client's legal problem.

The case that we will examine here involves a Vietnamese immigrant farmworker, Mr. Key. Mr. Key is a resident of the U.S. but he speaks no English. Unfortunately, he inadvertently overdosed on allergy medication because he could not read the warning label on the bottle; the warning label was printed only in English. As a result he took too much of the allergy medicine, and he became drowsy while driving a tractor. He fell off of the tractor, and was severely injured. He is suing LPC, the large pharmaceutical company that manufactured the drug, for failure to properly warn of the dangers of the drug. Mr. Key believes that LPC should have printed the warning label in Vietnamese as well as English. Mr. Key points out that LPC advertised the drug heavily over the radio in the Vietnamese language; this suggests that the company knew that many people in the Vietnamese community did not understand English. Nevertheless, they did not provide a written warning label in Vietnamese on the packaging of the allergy medication. Because Mr. Key lives in Nebraska, he filed his suit in a Nebraska state court. He is suing LPC for negligence. The relevant law in this case is the Nebraska state tort law of negligence. Mr. Key clams that, under Nebraska state tort law, LPC had a duty to print the warning label on its drug in Vietnamese.

With this background, read through the following excerpt from a memo written by an Associate at a law firm to a Partner. The purpose of this memo is to explain to the Partner whether Mr. Key's claim that LPC was negligent would be supported by the relevant law. As it turns out, the writer found no Nebraska court cases that specifically address this issue under Nebraska law. First, read the entire argument below. Then we will analyze specific parts of the memo [for the sake of simplicity, citations do not appear]:

Whether a manufacturer of a nonprescription drug is liable for failing to provide foreign language warning labels on a product that it markets to a specific language minority group in their native language, in this case Vietnamese, is a question of first impression in this jurisdiction. There are several cases in other states involving foreign language warning labels and product labels in general which may provide persuasive arguments to the Nebraska court.

The Supreme Court of California, in Ramirez v. Plough, held that manufacturers of nonprescription drugs are not liable for failing to provide foreign language warning labels for their products because state and federal statutory and administrative law does not require such.

LPC's warning labels satisfy all relevant state and federal law requirements, but that may not suffice if the Nebraska court adopts the federal appellate court's reasoning in Hubbard–Hall Chemical v Silverman, First Circuit. In this case, a manufacturer of a pesticide who complied with state and federal regulations but failed to provide foreign language warning labels was deemed liable after two semi-literate Puerto Rican laborers died after improperly using the manufacturer's product. The manufacturer's compliance with the regulations only served to satisfy interstate commerce requirements; the common law of Massachusetts, which was the law that the federal court applied, required a higher standard of care.

*The facts in our client's case are similar in nature to this case, but because no case law exists in Nebraska dealing with foreign language drug warning labels, the Nebraska courts have not adopted a legal standard with regard to state and federal regulations. Thus, it is **somewhat ambiguous** as to how the Nebraska court is likely to decide on this matter. If it employs the rationale of the Ramirez court, LPC **will most likely** prevail; if it follows the reasoning in Hubbard by requiring a higher standard than the one provided by the regulations, our client **will most likely** prevail.*

*The Ramirez court also declared that the defendant (the pharmaceutical company) was not liable for not providing foreign language warnings even though it advertised its product in Spanish and targeted the Spanish speaking community <u>because the plaintiff's mother, who administered the drug to the plaintiff, a minor, testified that she never saw or heard the defendant's advertisement for its product.</u> If the Nebraska court is persuaded by this decision, in order for our client to prevail, it **must be shown** that he was exposed to LPC's (the pharmaceutical company being sued) advertisements about the allergy medication prior to his use of it.*

Now let's look at specific sections of this text and evaluate its effectiveness using the CL Rubric. First, consider the first group of sentences in (1).

(1) *Whether a manufacturer of a nonprescription drug is liable for failing to provide foreign language warning labels on a product that it markets to a specific language minority group in their native language, in this case Vietnamese, is a question of first impression in this jurisdiction. There are several cases in other states involving foreign language warning labels and product labels in general which may provide persuasive jurisdiction for the Nebraska court.*

In these sentences, the writer lays out the status of the controlling law as it relates to the issues raised in the client's case. The writer notes that there are no prior Nebraska cases addressing this issue; this is what is meant by the phrase *"a question of first impression"*. The writer goes on to inform us that there are cases from other jurisdictions that the court might consider in making its decision. It is important for you to know that there are no prior decisions addressing foreign language warning labels that the Nebraska court is required to follow. Because the writer has no mandatory or binding authority from Nebraska courts to support his arguments, he must rely on the opinions of other courts. This often happens on a "case of first impression." Fortunately, courts in other states have addressed this issue and so the writer can use these court decisions to predict what a court in his state might do in a similar situation. Although the courts of Nebraska are not required to follow the decisions of other state or federal courts on a point of Nebraska law, decisions form other states could be persuasive to Nebraska courts.

The Common Law Argumentation follows in (2). (The sentences are labeled with letters for ease of explication):

(2) *a) The Supreme Court of California, in Ramirez v Plough, held
that manufacturers of nonprescription drugs are not liable for
failing to provide foreign language warning labels for their
products <u>because state and federal statutory and administrative
law does not require such.</u>*

*b) LPC's warning labels satisfy all relevant state and federal
law requirements, <u>but that may not suffice if the Nebraska court
adopts the federal appellate court's reasoning in Hubbard–Hall
Chemical v Silverman, which is a case from the First Circuit.</u>*

In the first half of sentence a, the writer presents the legally
significant finding of a prior case, *Ramirez* from the state court of
California. That court held that the pharmaceutical company was not
responsible for providing foreign language labels. This represents Step 1
in the CL Rubric, identifying a legally significant prior case and the key,
legally pertinent facts of that case. In the second half of the sentence, the
section that is underlined, we find the reasoning the *Ramirez* court used
to reach its decision, i.e. that the federal, state, and administrative laws
did not require such labeling. This represents Step 2 in CL Rubric,
identification of the court's reasoning.

The first half of sentence b provides the salient facts from the
client's case, reminding us that, just as the pharmaceutical company in
the *Ramirez* case, LPC's labeling complies with the state and federal
statutes. Even though the comparison is implicit, this represents Step 3
in the CL Rubric as the information is simple enough for the reader to
easily compare facts between the two cases on this point.

The second half of sentence b, the underlined section, does two
things. It gives a partial prediction about the court's possible ruling,
saying that simply satisfying the statutes may not be enough (and hence
the inference that the court *might* rule in the client's favor), and
introduces a second case, *Hubbard–Hall Chemical v Silverman*, which
counters the *Ramirez* case. This represents Step 4 and the beginnings of
a second Common Law Argument. *Hubbard–Hall Chemical* is a federal
appellate case from the First Circuit; as with *Ramirez*, the Nebraska
court is not obligated to follow it. Now let's look at the next section of
the memo in (3).

(3) *c) In this case, a manufacturer of a pesticide who complied with
state and federal regulations but failed to provide foreign language warning labels was deemed liable after two semi-literate
Puerto Rican laborers died after improperly using the manufacturer's product.*

Sentence c provides a more detailed account of the facts of *Hubbard–
Hall Chemical v. Silverman*, as well as information about the court's
ruling. A particularly important piece of information is that the common
law of Massachusetts has established a higher standard for warning
labels than the minimum laid out in the federal and administrative
statutes. This represents Step 1. Now consider sentence d in (4) below.

(4) *d) The manufacturer's compliance with the regulations only served to satisfy interstate commerce requirements; the common law of Massachusetts, which was the law that the federal court applied, required a higher standard of care.*

Sentence d provides us with the court's reasoning—even though the manufacturer complied with the standard set by federal statute, the court ruled that this was not sufficient. Instead, the court applied the common law from the state of Massachusetts, which set higher requirements for foreign language warnings. This represents Step 2. The argument progresses with sentences e, f, and g in (5).

(5) *e) The facts in our client's case are similar in nature to this case, but because no case law exists in Nebraska dealing with foreign language drug warning labels, the Nebraska courts have not adopted a legal standard with regard to state and federal regulations.*

*f) Thus, it is **somewhat ambiguous** as to how the Nebraska court is likely to decide on this matter.*

*g) If it employs the rationale of the Ramirez court, LPC **will most likely** prevail; if it follows the reasoning in Hubbard by requiring a higher standard than the one provided by the regulations, our client **will most likely** prevail.*

Sentence e provides a direct comparison between the client's case and *Hubbard–Hall Chemical*. Thus, this represents Step 3 in the CL Rubric. The second half of sentence e and sentences f, and g provide the writer's assessment of how the court might rule. Since there is no Nebraska case law dealing with the issue and the existing law from other jurisdictions does not provide a clear, consistent precedent, it is particularly difficult to predict how the court will rule. Notice that the writer is careful to warn the Partner of the difficulty in making a prediction by using phrases such as *is **somewhat ambiguous*** and ***will most likely.***

Now consider the text in (6).

(6) *h) The Ramirez court also declared that the defendant (the pharmaceutical company) was not liable for not providing foreign language warnings even though it advertised its product in Spanish and targeted the Spanish speaking community <u>because the plaintiff's mother</u>, who administered the drug to the plaintiff, a minor, testified that she never saw or heard the defendant's advertisement for its product.*

*i) If the Nebraska court is persuaded by this decision, in order for our client to prevail, **it must be shown** that he was exposed to LPC's (the pharmaceutical company being sued) advertisements about the allergy medication prior to his use of it.*

With sentence h, the writer is starting another Common Law Argument; notice it again draws on the *Ramirez* case. The writer intertwines Steps 1 and 2 of the argument. We find out the additional, salient facts that the company in the *Ramirez* case used foreign language advertising; however, the plaintiff testified that she did not see the ads. We also find out the court's reasoning in relationship to these particular facts. Even though the company advertised in Spanish, and thus implicitly recognized that many of its potential customers could not understand English, since the plaintiff was not exposed to the advertising, in this particular situation the company was judged not to have the additional obligation to provide written warnings in Spanish.

In sentence i the writer interweaves Step 3 and 4, making a hedged prediction about how the Nebraska court *might* rule on the client's case, if it is persuaded by the reasoning in the *Ramirez* case. The writer explicitly states the facts the law firm *must* show for this aspect of the *Ramierz* case to be helpful to the client.

Now consider another argument concerning the Nebraska case, which appears in (7) below. As you read this argument, ask yourself whether the writer has made arguments that would be accceptable to a U.S. audience:

> (7) *LPC targeted the Vietnamese community with special foreign language advertising. This clearly shows that LPC knew that many of their Vietnamese customers could not understand English. Moreover, they specifically encouraged their Vietnamese customers with allergy symptoms to use their product. Understanding this population's lack of English and having made the decision to advertise over the radio in Vietnamese, LPC had a moral obligation to also provide written warnings about the potential dangers of the drug. When he suffered allergy symptoms, our client took the drug he had heard advertised on the radio in his native language. Because he was not given any warnings in Vietnamese, he didn't know the appropriate dosage and consequently was so severely injured that he will not be able to return to work as a farm laborer. This is clearly an unjust situation and should provide persuasive evidence to support our client's claims.*

Careful examination of the excerpt in (7) reveals that the writer has forcefully put forward a particular interpretation of the facts of the case and asserted an obligation on the part of LPC. This argument is based on an everyday, common sense notion of what is just. In discussions and speeches outside the courtroom, many people may be swayed by the argument. However, it is not acceptable Common Law Argumentation. The lawyer writing this memo must discuss previous cases and the court's reasoning in those cases, even if they are not binding on the Nebraska court, which will provide a legal basis for the Nebraska court to establish LPC's legal obligation to provide foreign language warnings. Judges in the U.S. system cannot impose a new legal obligation based simply on the lawyer's logic. Passionate, common sense arguments may win cases on television, but in real U.S. courts, establishing a chain of logic between the facts and reasoning used in prior case law to your client's case is what is required.

2.8.3 CL Rubric Exercise

Now consider another excerpt from another memo concerning the Nebraska case in (8). In this excerpt the writer is introducing argumentation based on his reading of Oregon state law. The writer is trying to make a prediction about what a Nebraska court might rule in Mr. Key's case by making analogies to decisions of Oregon courts in similar situations. Please read the argument and see if you can identify the four components of the CL Rubric:

(8) *As a consumer of the allergy medication, one could argue that our client was protected by a special relationship, that of a manufacturer to his consumer. The Oregon Supreme Court found that a prescription drug manufacturer has a duty to warn doctors of any dangerous side effects. Ocksenholt v Lederle Laboratories. The court was concerned with protecting patients (the ultimate consumers of any drug) from harmful side-effects and wanted to ensure that physicians would have access to all relevant information so that they could relate it to their patients. Both the physician in Ocksenholt and our client were consumers of a manufacturer's drug. As consumers, both had to rely on the manufacturer for information. Lacking the schooling of a physician, our client was even more dependent on the safety information than the doctor. In light of this and if the Nebraska is persuaded by the standards set by the Oregon courts, the Nebraska court might find that a drug manufacturer owes an equal, if not greater, duty to consumers it targets with special foreign language advertising who are outside of the medical profession.*

After you have analyzed the excerpt, go to the COURSE MATERIALS section of your TWEN site and click on the item labeled Chapter 2: Using the Common Law (CL) Rubric. Compare your analysis to the one given there. Once you are satisfied that you understand the analysis, you are ready to read the law review article.

2.9 CLOSE READING EXERCISE 2: THE LAW REVIEW ARTICLE

Now it's time for you to gather background information on the case by closely reading the article that the Partner sent to you in his email. Please read the law review article, *Exit Consents in Sovereign Bond Exchanges*, which appears in the COURSE MATERIALS section of your TWEN site. As you read it, think about what the Partner has told you about your client. You know that you are interested in the rights and obligations of a sovereign, Urbania, and you are interested in the process of restructuring sovereign bonds of some kind. When you do any sort of research, it is important to have a situation in mind. You are more likely to pay attention to reading material if you are reading it for a purpose— to find an answer; to confirm a suspicion; to develop an argument. Your reading will be much more efficient than it would have been if the Partner had not sent that simple e-mail.

As you read the article, also keep the CL Rubric in mind. Look for sections of the article in which the authors use Common Law Argumentation. You will find that a good deal of their presentation does not directly involve Common Law Argumentation, but some key points do. Try to identify them. Your reading task, then, involves at least two layers—(1) to gather background information and understand the content presented in the article and (2) to pay attention to how the argument is constructed. We call this second type of reading, "reading like a writer." The point is that if you remain alert to the elements of Common Law Argumentation as you read legal documents, you will become more and more familiar with how this very important part of U.S. Legal Discourse works. Often, we read only for information and do not pay attention to the form of the argument. So, you might read excellent examples of the style or form of writing that helps create what U.S. lawyers understand as U.S. Legal Discourse, but because you are not paying attention, the examples do not become a part of your knowledge that can be accessed when you begin to try to write like a U.S. lawyer.

As you read this article, be aware that you are reading it to learn something about the sovereign debt area of the law, to find primary law that might help you to address your client's problem, and to learn about USLD and how lawyers organize documents and use English.

2.10 INTRODUCTION TO LEGAL CITATION

Legal Citation is part of U.S. Legal Discourse. Because of the importance of precedent and the necessity of supporting legal arguments by relevant authority, lawyers always cite[1] the authority that they are using to support their arguments. The reason that they cite the authority is so other lawyers (and the courts) can find the authority themselves and read it to evaluate the relevance of the authority and whether the writer has characterized the source accurately. Citation, then, is used to convey several messages. Let's look at the citation for the article that you are about to read.[2]

Lee C. Buchheit and Mitu Gulati, Exit Consents in Sovereign Bond Exchanges, 48 UCLA L. Rev. 59 (2000).

If you go to your TWEN site, and click the tab marked Westlaw Research, you will notice that there is a place where you can type a citation and Westlaw will take you to the document. Notice that in the top left corner of the first page of the article, Westlaw has printed "Cite as 48 UCLA L. Rev. 59." You can always use that citation to find the document on

---

1. "Cite" is a verb that was formed from the noun, "citation." Often in USLD, we speak of "citing authority." It simply means to tell the reader what source you are using to support your argument. We don't think this word has general usage in English.

2. All documents that we will use this semester have the relevant parts of the citation indicated on the top of the document. In most cases, you will not need to look further than to the front or back cover of the Bluebook to find the citation form that you need.

Westlaw. The citation tells you that the article is in volume 48 of the UCLA Law Review, and the article begins on page 59 of that volume. If you were to go to your law school's library, you could find a hard copy of this article on the shelf. The bound volumes (books) containing the UCLA Law Reviews would be arranged in numerical order. You could go to Volume 48, and, on page 59 of that volume, you would find this article.

All citation follows this format. When we begin to look for case law, the citations to cases will refer to the volumes of the books in the library that contain the cases. The citation system for legal sources, of course, was developed long before there were computers. Because so few lawyers now actually do legal research using books from the library, it is an odd historical fact that our citation system is based on the location of materials in books. When you return to your home countries, it is unlikely that you will have access to a library that contains all of the books that contain all of the legal sources that you may need to read. However, by using the Westlaw "Cite as" citations, you can find just about everything you need.

Chapter 3

SCHOLARLY DISCOURSE
ABOUT THE LAW

3.1 INTRODUCTION

Now that you have met your client and you have read the Gulati/Buchheit law review article, you are beginning to understand the legal issues involved in your case. In this Chapter, we will look carefully at this law review article and will evaluate its role in the Legal Discourse about sovereign bond restructuring. Any Legal Discourse is made up of many kinds of texts. Scholarly texts, such as the Gulati/Buchheit article, have a specific role to play. The role that they play may be quite different from the role that scholarly texts play in your own legal systems. Part of learning about a discourse is learning how the various participants in that discourse treat different texts in different situations. Our discussion here is devoted to the legal significance of scholarly texts.

The full text of the article is available from a link in the COURSE MATERIALS section of your TWEN site. We will be referring to specific sections of the article here. As you read this Chapter, please have a copy of the article in front of you—either in print or electronic form.

3.2 TEXTUAL ANALYSIS OF A LAW REVIEW ARTICLE

Any document, including any legal document, is written from a point of view. In addition to conveying information about an area of the law, the law review article that you have read reflects the authors' opinions about how the law in this area should work. If you searched Westlaw for other law review articles on this topic, you would find articles written by other authors, and these articles would reflect the opinions of their authors. The function of scholarly discourse is very different from the function of other types of texts in Legal Discourse. For example, the *Erie v. Tompkins* text that you read at the end of Chapter 1 is an opinion of the United States Supreme Court. The function of that opinion was to decide a legal issue and to give specific guidance that all future federal courts that are ruling on the same or similar issues must follow. The writer of the opinion, Justice Brandeis, has a duty to read and evaluate all relevant prior cases and to decide the case in a way that conforms to the prevailing law. In the next Chapter, we will evaluate other cases that specifically address the specific legal issues that the Urbania case presents. Those cases, like the *Erie* case, are written by judges who are bound by prior precedent. Judges make arguments that are consistent with that precedent and guide future judges to make consistent rulings.

Scholars have different incentives from judges. Scholars are sometimes simply trying to make provocative arguments. The extent to which they make sound legal arguments is a function of how they want to be viewed in the scholarly legal community. If a scholar makes novel and non-obvious contributions to the knowledge base in his area of the law, he has written a successful article. Evaluating a scholarly article is very different, however, from evaluating a court opinion. In this Chapter, we will examine whether the authors of this law review article have successfully achieved the goals of scholarly Legal Discourse. As an LL.M. student, you may have the opportunity to participate in scholarly discourse as well. For example, when you write papers for your seminar classes, you will be expected to make a valuable contribution legal literature. As we evaluate the contribution made by this law review article, you should become more aware of the kinds of papers that you will be expected to write for your LL.M. seminars.

3.2.1   The Author Must Have a Valuable and Novel Thesis

The authors of this article have a very specific purpose. They intend to show that countries that find themselves in financial troubles may have an option to restructure their sovereign bonds that may not have occurred to them before. The thesis of this paper is that courts applying New York law will not penalize countries that use exit consents to "encourage" bondholders to participate in restructurings of sovereign bond issues. This is an excellent example of a scholarly thesis. The authors have suggested a novel and prescriptive solution to a problem that they have identified. Legal scholarship in the U.S. Legal Discourse Community must do more than describe a phenomenon; it must identify a problem and offer a solution to it.

We can evaluate this legal text by examining how well it meets the expectations of the U.S. legal audience. The U.S. legal reader expects that a scholarly paper—whether it is a law review article or an LL.M. seminar paper—will meet the following criteria:

(1) The paper will make a novel and non-obvious claim.

(2) The paper will demonstrate that the author has done adequate research.

(3) The paper will offer a conclusion that is useful to the legal community.[1]

---

1. For a full discussion about how law students can write good scholarly papers, see Eugene Volokh, Writing a Student Article, 48 J. Legal Educ. 342 (1996). Volokh's

3.2.2   The Author Will Have a Point of View

In addition to expecting that a scholarly paper will satisfy the criteria mentioned above, the U.S. legal audience expects that a scholarly article will express the author's point of view. The purpose of writing a scholarly article is, in part, to stimulate discussion in the legal community. Scholars are not judges (and some judges are not scholars). Scholars are not bound by precedent, and they do not expect that their writings will bind future courts. Legal scholarship is the essence of persuasive authority. That is, as opposed to court opinions, which contribute to the substance of the common law and which must be followed by other courts that they bind, legal scholarship is simply a suggestion to the Legal Discourse Community of an interesting idea that other scholars, lawyers, and judges might want to consider.

Sometimes, scholars do influence courts with their writings. In fact, some scholars write their articles with the specific intention of persuading courts (and lawyers who make arguments to courts) that their point of view should be the law of the land. As we have mentioned earlier, Justice Brandeis mentioned a scholar's work whose point of view was similar to the Justice's on the issue of the Tyson doctrine. Perhaps the scholar's paper was persuasive to the Justice, or perhaps it simply corresponded to the position that the Justice arrived at independently. In either case, scholars present an important voice in U.S. Legal Discourse. Nevertheless, when you evaluate any scholarly article, you must remember that it represents the scholar's opinion and point of view. It does not have the force of law.

3.3   ANALYZING THE STRUCTURE OF THE SCHOLARLY ARTICLE

Understanding the expectations of their legal audience, successful scholars specifically structure their articles in anticipation of those expectations. Notice that the Gulati/Buchheit article is structured extremely well. Let's look at how the authors used the structure of their article to assure the legal audience that they had written a successful scholarly paper.[2]

3.3.1   The Abstract

The paper begins with a short abstract. The abstract serves several functions. First, it tells the reader what the paper is about. In addition,

article is focused on the mechanics of writing a paper. My focus here is on how the U.S. legal audience uses scholarly papers in making legal arguments. Nevertheless, we draw on many of Volokh's insights in this Chapter. A link to Professor Volokh's article appears in a tab marked "Chapter 3: Writing a Student Article" in the COURSE MATERIALS on your TWEN SITE.

2.   Although there are many ways that a scholarly paper can be structured, and some structures are better suited to some topics than others, you might consider using this structure when you write your LL.M. seminar papers. At the very least, it would be useful to consider whether this structure would work for you as a way of intentionally focusing on the choice of structure as an important element in writing your paper.

it tells the reader what the author's point of view on the subject will be. It is quite clear what the authors believe about the issues that they discuss in their article. Notice that the authors refer negatively to bondholders who they call "holdouts" in the first paragraph of the abstract.[3] Moreover, they say that "Holdouts pose a litigation threat to the sovereign and may even jeopardize the sovereign's ability to service the new bonds it has issued to the other creditors participating in the exchange."[4]

The second paragraph of the abstract sets out the authors' mission in writing the paper. They want to offer a solution to a problem that they have identified in the sovereign bond area of the law. By doing this, the authors have satisfied one of the main expectations that the U.S. legal reader will have. U.S. legal readers want to know what the authors will contribute to the collective knowledge of lawyers who practice in the sovereign bond area and scholars who write about it. The authors say that they are offering a new "less radical" solution to a perceived problem.[5] It is only the authors' point of view, but it can be quite helpful to judges or other lawyers who may be thinking about similar legal issues.

3.3.2 Using the Table of Contents to Evaluate the Usefulness of the Article

This article contains a helpful Table of Contents following the abstract. This is not common in U.S. law review articles, but it can be quite useful. By looking at the Table of Contents, you can decide whether you want to read the whole article or whether you would rather read the most relevant parts. Because this article is relatively short and because the Partner asked you to read it (as did your professor), you will probably want to read the whole thing. The Table of Contents lists the various subject headings throughout the article. Notice that the items listed in the Table of Contents correspond directly to the subject headings throughout the paper. Most law review articles (and many legal documents in general) contain helpful subject headings. Even if this article did not have a Table of Contents, you could simply skim the subject headings throughout the paper to see what topics the authors are discussing.

Using subject headings is very common in U.S. Legal Discourse. For example, when judges write legal opinions, they often use subject headings in the text to help the reader identify relevant parts of the text. You will notice this more in recent opinions. Justice Brandeis did not use subject headings in his *Erie v. Tompkins* opinion. As you read more recent cases, try to notice whether the writer has used these headings. If the writer does use them, ask yourself whether they are helpful to you. Later in the book, when we are discussing typical legal memorandums

---

3. Mitu Gulati and Lee Buchheit, Exit Consents in Sovereign Bond Exchanges, 48 UCLA L. Rev. 59 (2000).

4. Id.

5. Id.

written by Associates at law firms, we will again talk about subject headings. When lawyers write a legal memorandum, they often use subject headings to alert the reader to the topics that they will discuss. Using subject headings throughout a text is quite common in U.S. Legal Discourse. Because the subject headings help the reader to follow the writer's arguments, using subject headings in your writing will help you to write a paper that meets the reader's expectations.

3.3.3 The Author Sets Out His Point of View in the Introduction

Notice the language in the Introduction. The authors use language that shows their point of view. For example, in the first paragraph, the authors point out that the "official sector ... have made it clear"[6] that bondholders should not expect to be "bailed out"[7] if sovereigns cannot fulfill their obligations under their bonds. The authors try to make it seem obvious that the only choice bondholders have is to allow the sovereign to reduce or restructure its debt to the bondholders.

With that as background, in the next paragraph, the authors use very positive language to describe the "large majority of bondholders."[8] These bondholders "can be expected to participate in such reschedulings."[9] The authors use less flattering language for the bondholders who "refuse to participate."[10] These bondholders are said to be "demanding preferential payouts."[11] Later in the paragraph, these bondholders who refuse to be good participants are characterized as "maverick creditors"[12] and accused of "delaying, derailing or exploiting"[13] the plans of the participating bondholders. These words have negative connotations in English and they emphasize the authors' point of view. Just by reading the Introduction, one quickly understands that bondholders who participate in reschedulings are "good" and those that refuse to participate are "bad."

The final paragraph of the Introduction gives you a clear view about the authors' goals for the paper. They present their idea as a "less radical"[14] alternative solution to the sovereign debt problems than those that they have mentioned earlier. Having a "less radical" solution is always perceived as better and more practical than having a "radical" solution. Again, the authors use language carefully and intentionally in ways that entice the reader to want to agree with their view.

In Parts A and B of the Introduction, the authors accomplish one of the major tasks of legal scholarship: they identify a legal problem. The authors have chosen to demonstrate this problem with an example. By focusing on the fictitious country of Ruritania, that authors have chosen a common narrative device. It is easier for readers to think about

6. Id. at 60.
7. Id.
8. Id.
9. Id.
10. Id.

11. Id.
12. Id. at 61.
13. Id.
14. Id. at 62.

abstract concepts by referring to concrete examples. Using examples is very common in U.S. Legal Discourse, and the authors here use their example well. Sometimes, you will be addressing an actual fact situation, and so you will not need to invent an example. Nonetheless, it is important to notice that the concrete example does make the substance of the paper easier to understand.

3.3.4   Building Background Knowledge: The Literature Review

Section I of the paper is called "Exit Consents." In this section, the authors first give a brief summary of their proposal for using exit consents in sovereign bond exchanges. The summary contains no citations to any legal authority supporting the proposal. This opening paragraph is intended only to set the stage for the legal arguments that the authors will give in the following sections.

The sections labeled A and B constitute the authors' review of what they believe to be the relevant legal literature on the subject of exit consents. As you read these sections, notice that the authors cite no primary legal authority. That is the authors offer no analysis of any cases from federal or state courts that involve the issues that they intend to address in their paper. Nearly every footnote in these two sections is to another scholarly paper—one, in fact, was written by one of the authors. These sections do not give the reader any clear picture of how a court applying New York law might rule on the issue of using exit consents in either the private or sovereign sector. Nonetheless, the authors have given their view of what scholars have generally said about related issues. In this case, given that the authors have offered no court interpretations of the relevant New York law as it applies to exit consents, a legal reader might want to know more about what courts have said about similar issues.

If the reader wanted to know more about the role of the courts in this debate, he could simply read the articles that the authors cite to see if any of them discusses the applicable law. In fairness to the authors, we could accept these sections as simply the authors' characterization of what scholars have said on these issues. The legal reader, however, expects some analysis of the applicable law in the paper. Let us continue through the article to see if the authors present this in alter sections.

3.3.5   Analyzing Analogous Case Law

Section C seems to be the complement to Sections A and B. In Section C, the authors discuss what they call the "leading case on exit consents."[15] The case they have chosen is *Katz v. Oak Industries.*[16] In fact, the majority of the legal analysis in the paper concerns the *Katz* case. Recall that the thesis of the paper concerns whether courts applying New York law would view favorably a country's use of exit consents

---

15. Id. at 70.

16. Katz v. Oak Industries, 508 A. 2d 873 (Del. Ch. 1986).

in sovereign bond exchanges. Let's examine what the legal reader might infer from the choice of *Katz* as the "leading case."

3.3.5.1   Evaluating a Legal Citation

By looking at the citation to the *Katz* case, you can learn many things. Let's look at the citation more carefully; the full citation appears in (1) below:

(1) *Katz v. Oak Industries*,[17] 508 A.2d 873 (Del. Ch. 1986).

The name of the case comes before the first comma. This is followed by the alpha-numeric citation that you would type into Westlaw to find the case. The "A. 2d" refers to a series of books in the library called the Atlantic Reporter, 2nd Series. This series of books collects the state court cases in one group of states, called the Atlantic states, which have been reported to the publisher. The states in the Atlantic states are: New Jersey, Delaware, Pennsylvania, Maryland, and the District of Columbia. The symbol, A.2d, tells the reader that this is a case from a state court from one of those states. The numbers tell you that this case is in volume 508 of the series and is reported beginning on page 873 of that volume. The information in the parentheses is particularly useful. The symbol, Del. Ch., means that this case was decided by the Delaware Chancery Court.

There are other things you need to know about the *Katz* case as well. What law was the court applying? Delaware law? New York law? If it is a Delaware court applying Delaware law, how relevant is this case to your question of New York law? If it is a Delaware court applying New York law, it might be more relevant, but not at all binding[18] on New York courts.[19] In addition, you must look at the specific facts of the *Katz* case. How different is a corporate case from a sovereign case? What were the exact facts of *Katz*. What was the exact holding? What can you infer from this case about how a New York court would rule on your issue?

The authors leave a lot of work for the reader to do. First, if you were trying to determine whether you accepted the authors' conclusions in this article, you would have to read the *Katz* case yourself to answer these questions. You could not simply use *Katz* as support for an argument that exit consents are legally valid based only on the assertions of the authors of this article. *Katz* merely stands for the proposition

---

17. Case names in citations can either be underlined or italicized. We prefer italics. You may do either; however, you should be consistent throughout your document. See The Bluebook, Rule 10.

18. Binding is a term of art meaning that a court of lesser ranking must follow the case holding. For example, opinions on New York law of the Court of Appeals of New York are "binding" on all lower courts. Similarly, opinions on federal law of the United States Supreme Court are "binding" on the lower federal courts.

19. In an attempt to strengthen the relevance of the *Katz* case, the authors specifically mention the judge in the case, Chancellor Allen. They do this because Chancellor Allen is a very famous contract law scholar, who currently teaches at NYU Law School. In general, it is not at all relevant who the judge is in a case, and it is quite uncommon to mention the judge by name in writing. Courts refer to other courts and not to specific judges. It is the court, and not the judge himself, who has authority.

that this particular exit consent in this particular context was deemed by this court to be valid under the law applied. In order to properly evaluate the claims that these authors make, you would need to do some research of your own.

Recall, however, that the authors say that they are interested in New York law and the opinions of New York courts. A legal reader might ask why the authors chose this case to focus on. In fact, the authors of the Article say at the end of their discussion of *Katz*:

> Although New York courts have also noted Chancellor Allen's discussion of bondholder rights in Katz with approval, [FN49] they have rarely had occasion explicitly to consider the legal validity of exit consents. There are good grounds, however, for believing that New York courts would follow the lead of the Delaware case law in this area.[20]

If you look in Footnote 49 in their article, the authors have cited one case: *United States v. Jolly.* The full citation to this case appears in (2) below.

> (2) *United States v. Jolly,* 102 F.3rd 46, 48 (2nd Cir. 1996) (citing Katz).

Let's look at the citation to this case to evaluate its eventual usefulness in deciding the issue that the authors present. From the citation, you can tell that this is reported in a book called the F.3rd. This is the third series of a group of volumes that reports cases from the federal appeals courts. Just like the A.2d series, the F.3rd series can be found in your law school's law library. In volume 102 of that series, on page 46, you would find the beginning of the case, *United States v. Jolly.* Notice that the citation contains two page numbers. The second page number refers to the page on which the particular information that the author has mentioned appears in the text of the case (here, "Although New York courts have also noted Chancellor Allen's discussion of bondholder rights in Katz with approval"). Whenever you mention a particular holding or refer to some specific language in another source, whether it is directly quoted or not, you must cite to the specific page or pages where it appears in the text. Remember, one of the main reasons that lawyers cite to other material is so help other lawyers to evaluate their claims. Giving specific page numbers helps readers find information quickly.

Looking into the parentheses of this citation, we learn that this case is from the Second Circuit Court of Appeals, a federal court that includes the federal courts in the states of New York and Connecticut. Given this citation, we still have some questions about the relevance of this case. First of all, we do not know which federal court in the Second Circuit ruled on the *Jolly* case, nor do we know what law that court was applying. Is it a court in New York that might be thought to be familiar with issues of New York law? Is the court actually applying New York

---

20. Id. at 73.

law? Also, because this is a federal court opinion, its rulings on matters of state law are not binding on the state courts. Even if this were a federal court in New York, and even if it were applying New York law, the highest New York state court, New York Court of Appeals, is not bound by this ruling. Recall from your reading of *Erie v. Tompkins*, that a federal court applying state law must defer to the highest state court in its interpretation of the state's law. Again, this article does not answer all of the questions that we might have in addressing our Urbania case. You would have to read the *Jolly* case yourself in order to determine whether it will be helpful in solving the Urbania case. The *Jolly* case and the *Katz* case are available in the COURSE MATERIALS tab on your TWEN site.

To critically evaluate the usefulness (and the validity) of the authors' statements about these cases, you should read them, and determine how accurate the authors' statements are. For example, when reading the *Jolly* case, ask yourself the following questions: Does this case simply refer to *Katz*? Does the case endorse the specific ruling of *Katz*? How is *Katz* discussed in this case? Notice that the authors admit that the specific legal question—the legal validity of exit consents under New York law—has ''rarely'' been explicitly considered by the New York courts.[21] The authors have given you some very useful background information about the history of exit consents; they have also done some good initial research for you by finding a couple of cases and discussing them from their point of view. In order to fully evaluate their claims, however, a legal reader would have to read the cases and come to his own conclusions.

3.3.5.2   Evaluating a Legal Argument

Notice what the authors have said in their text about the *Jolly* case. ''Although New York courts have also noted Chancellor Allen's discussion of bondholder rights in *Katz* with approval . . .''[22] Given the authors' view that exit consents are valid under New York law, they want to make their citation of *Jolly* seem as strong as possible. The Second Circuit is not strictly a New York court; it is a federal court that sits in New York. As you recall from your reading of the *Erie* case, federal courts must choose which state law to apply when they are deciding cases based on state law. In fact, when applying a state's law, the federal courts must follow the precedent of that state's highest court. For federal courts applying New York law, it is important for them to follow precedent of the New York courts. Because federal courts in the Second Circuit so often decide cases under New York law, federal courts in the Second Circuit often cite to other federal courts of that circuit when deciding issues of New York law. Although the cases of the New York Court of Appeals (the highest state court in New York) are binding precedent. On all state courts and federal courts on state law issues,

---

21. Id. at 73.   **22.** Gulati at 73.

decisions of the federal courts of the Second Circuit are highly persuasive on New York state law issues.

The authors of this article are asking the reader to make an additional leap from binding authority. Recall, again, that the authors are claiming that the *Katz* case would be highly persuasive to New York courts on the issue of exit consents in sovereign bond exchanges. Because the *Katz* case is from a Delaware state court (not even the highest Delaware state court) applying Delaware law, the reader should be somewhat skeptical of the authors' claim. The authors use *Jolly*, a Second Circuit case, to try to argue that *Katz* should be persuasive to New York courts. The authors take great care to point out that the court in *Jolly* "noted Chancellor Allen's discussion of bondholder rights in *Katz* with approval." *Id.*

The authors' intended this reference to *Jolly* to show that New York courts (at least one federal court applying New York law) seemed to look favorably on the reasoning in *Katz*. Because the authors would like the reasoning of *Katz* to be adopted by the New York courts if they were to consider exit consents in sovereign bond exchanges, it would help their argument if they could show that some New York court had in fact adopted the *Katz* reasoning. The best that they can offer is their citation in *Jolly*. This is a rather vague and weak showing of support. You must read *Jolly* to evaluate this claim. A "discussion of bondholder rights in Katz"[23] is a rather broad description. Which rights discussed in *Katz* are the authors talking about? Rights given by New York law? The same rights that you are interested in for your Urbania case? Again, the authors invoke the name of Chancellor Allen in an attempt to give added support to their claim. This sort of argumentation is understandable in the context of a scholarly article where the authors are trying to support a particular point of view; however, this particular argument is weaker than the Common Law Arguments that judges typically use in their decisions.

Sometimes courts will refer to law review articles as sources of information. For example, as we saw in the *Erie v. Tompkins* case, Justice Brandeis cited an article from the Harvard Law Review to lend further support to his analysis of the law:

> But it was the more recent research of a competent scholar, who examined the original document, which established that the construction given to it by the Court was erroneous; and that the purpose of the section was merely to make certain that, in all matters except those in which some federal law is controlling, the federal courts exercising jurisdiction in diversity of citizenship cases would apply as their rules of decision the law of the state, unwritten as well as written.[24]

23. Id.

24. *Erie v. Tompkins*, 304 U.S. 641 (1938) (Citing Charles Warren, New Light on the History of the Federal Judiciary Act of 1789, 37 Harv.L.Rev. 49, 51–52, 81–88, 108 (1923)).

Notice that Justice Brandeis did not use this article as "precedent" in his argument. He simply noted that scholars had researched the issue of whether the Tyson doctrine was consistent with the Federal Judiciary Act of 1789, and he asserted that this particular scholar had agreed with the Justice's conclusion. Justice Brandeis does not directly quote from the article. Rather, he summarizes the key points that he derived from the article, and he cites the specific places in the article where the author addresses the Tyson doctrine.

Justice Brandeis has used this law review article in an appropriate way. He has based his legal conclusions on his analysis of the prior case law, and he has added the additional information that some scholars agree with his view. This is the extent to which law review articles are typically used in common law argumentation.

In this Chapter, we have analyzed a law review article critically from the point of view of a legal reader interested in addressing a client's legal issue: that is, what would a New York courts have to say about Urbania's plan to use exit consents in its plan to restructure some of its sovereign debt. Although the article was extremely helpful in giving the reader some valuable background knowledge about the area of sovereign bond exchanges, the legal arguments in the article were not completely satisfying. We looked at some of the authors' arguments based on the *Katz* and *Jolly* cases in Sections A, B, and C of the article. With this discussion as background, now you can carefully re-read Sections D and E of the article. As you do, pay careful attention to how the authors use the authority they cite.

A law review article is an excellent source for primary law and for getting valuable perspectives on legal issues. You should always be aware, however, of the author's point of view when reading secondary sources such as law review articles. In U. S. Legal Discourse, a scholar's point of view is not legal precedent; judges may be persuaded by a scholar's article; however, they are only bound to follow the opinions of courts that bind them. In the next Chapter we will look closer at how judges analyze cases by referring to the rationales and the holdings of prior cases: that is, the Common Law Argumentation method.

3.4 CLOSE READING EXERCISE 3: WRITING A STUDENT ARTICLE

We have looked at the law review article, *Exit Consents in Sovereign Bond Exchanges,* from three somewhat different points of view; first, we used the article to get some very useful background information about sovereign bond exchanges; second, we used the article to focus on the authors' use of authority and contrasted the role of law review authors in U.S. Legal Discourse to the role of judges. Legal readers are wise to use law review articles for background information; however, they should rely on primary law when doing their own legal analysis.

The third point of view is a more practical one. Because it is likely you will be writing seminar papers as part of your LL.M. degree, we also looked at this law review article as an example that you could follow in structuring your own papers. Every year, LL.M. students write papers for their classes, and sometimes these students publish their papers in U.S. law reviews. As we have said here, the role of scholarly writing in U.S. Legal Discourse is perhaps different from the role of scholarly writing in the Legal Discourse that you are used to. In some academic cultures, scholars produce authoritative works that meticulously describe some specific area of the law. The purpose of those scholarly works is to provide clear and factual information that the participants in the Legal Discourse can rely on.

Although a legal reader can certainly learn a lot of valuable things from reading U.S.-style law review articles, their purpose is quite different. Legal scholars in the U.S. put a high value on innovative thinking. In fact, the law review article that we have read is quite innovative. It poses a problem, and it offers a creative way of addressing it. We saw that the authors' legal arguments could have been stronger, but the thesis of the paper was very engaging, and, as such, the paper was a successful law review article. As you begin to think about writing your own seminar papers, you must satisfy the expectations of the scholarly reader and adopt the conventions of the U.S. Legal Discourse Community.

Go to the COURSE MATERIALS section of your TWEN site and click the item called "Chapter 3: Writing a Student Article." This article describes the goals of scholarly writing in the U.S. and explains how you can become a participant in U.S. Legal Discourse. We will discuss more aspects of scholarly discourse in our next class.

Chapter 4

JUDICIAL DISCOURSE
AS THE LAW

4.1 INTRODUCTION

Now that you have some background knowledge about the area of the law that will affect your client's case, you are ready to look closely at some of the relevant court opinions that discuss these issues. Because the authors of the law review article had a point of view about the use of exit consents in sovereign bond exchanges, their analysis of the law was somewhat biased. Their bias was evident both in the ways they chose their language and in the way they chose which law they would analyze. The purpose of their law review article was to convince the reader that New York courts were likely to embrace their idea that exit consents could be used in sovereign bond exchanges.

As we saw in Chapter 3, the authors chose to focus on cases that they believed would support their argument. Although they certainly understood that New York courts (or federal courts applying New York law) would be the most authoritative on their issue, they focused on a Delaware state court case that served their purposes. As a critical reader of the law review article, you learned many things. First, you learned a little bit about how exit consents work. You also learned a little bit about the history of how countries issue sovereign debt. The authors presented each of those things fairly objectively. In order to critically evaluate the authors' legal arguments, however, you must read the relevant law yourselves. In this chapter, we will look closely at some of the relevant court cases and try to predict how a court applying New York law might rule on our client's particular case.

4.2 UNDERSTANDING THE JUDGE'S POINT OF VIEW

Just as authors of law review articles have a point of view, judges who write court opinions have their own rhetorical agendas. The purpose of a court opinion is to decide a case in controversy that has been put before the court. In a trial court case, the judge may hear testimony from witnesses and she may consider other types of evidence. If there is a jury, that jury decides the relevant issues of fact; if it is a trial without a jury, the judge will decide the disputed fact issues. Some of the cases you will read will come from federal district courts. Although these courts are strictly trial courts that hear testimony and weigh evidence, many of the cases that you will read will be in the court on purely legal issues. The parties may have stipulated in advance that there are no disputes about the factual issues in the case. The question before the court is one of how to apply the current law to those undisputed facts. In those cases, the trial court makes a legal ruling very much like the rulings that an appellate court makes.

When reading a trial court opinion, such as the opinion of a federal district court, you should pay careful attention to what the judge is doing. In general, the judge will first set out a legal question. The legal question will focus on a specific body of law—statutory law, common law, or a combination of the two—that applies to a specific set of facts. Once the judge has framed the legal issues and highlighted the legally significant facts, she will carefully analyze opinions of other courts that have ruled on similar issues. It is important for you to pay attention to what the judge says about the case she is deciding and how the case is the same or different from the cases she discusses. Sometimes, a judge is not as precise about this analysis as you might expect. Remember, the judge's job is to decide the case. She may give an extensive explanation of her decision, or she may simply cite some prior decisions and quickly decide the issue in her case. It is the lawyer's job (your job) to think carefully about what her analysis must have been given the conclusion that she reached and the cases that she cited.

Appellate court judges will do the same sort of analysis. Often, the specific issue that the appellate court will address is whether the trial court below decided its case correctly. If the trial court made findings of fact, those factual findings generally will be given great deference by the appellate court. The appellate court will focus its analysis on whether the trial court's legal analysis was consistent with existing precedent. This task of critically reading a court opinion is one of the most challenging and the most intellectually satisfying aspect of Common Law Argumentation.

4.3   UNDERSTANDING THE JUDGE'S AUDIENCE

The audience to which the judge writes his opinion is varied. First, the judge is addressing the parties to the dispute. He must focus on the specific legal issue or issues that the parties have brought before him, and he must give a final opinion about the law as it applies to the facts in that case. In addition to the parties, however, the judge's audience includes other judges. One of the purposes of the opinion, in addition to settling the dispute between the parties, is to restate the law in a new context. As the judge applies the common law to the facts before him, he will refer to other cases in which judges have decided similar legal issues.

The judge's discussion of these cases supports his decision in the case before him. He is trying to assure the legal community that he has considered the relevant existing case law and that he has decided this case in a way that "fits" with those prior cases. A good judge will choose cases that have similar facts to his case; he will explain the similarities and differences between those cases and his case; and he will explain which facts distinguish his case from the prior cases. Applying the law as it has been announced in the prior cases, he will ultimately decide the case before him.

As you read court opinions, you must always remember what the judge is doing; he is simultaneously speaking to two audiences: the parties to the case and to the Legal Discourse community, including judges and other lawyers. As you evaluate the legal memorandums in the next Chapter, you will be looking for the writers to do something quite similar to what the judges do in legal opinions. You will look to see that the writer has cited cases from relevant courts that discuss similar legal issues to those of the client. In trying to predict what a New York court would say about the client's case, you will look for the writer to discuss similar cases and compare them to the client's case. In this Chapter, we will look at how one judge has done this.

4.4 PERFORMING A CLOSE READING OF A COURT OPINION

Sometimes, you will have a case that is "on point"—that is, a case that appears to address the legal issues that affect your client's case. For example, the Exit Consent article that we discussed in the last Chapter focused on *Katz v. Oak Industries, Inc.* Although the *Katz* case appears to be factually similar to our Urbania case in some ways, we must determine how valuable the case would be in the particular Legal Discourse that surrounds our client's case. Remember, we are interested in finding cases that will be persuasive to New York courts on issues of New York law that address the issue of whether a sovereign could be liable to some of its bondholders for actions that it is contemplating. Although it appears to be factually similar to our client's case, *Katz* is about a corporate issuer of bonds, and it is the opinion of a court in Delaware; it might not be persuasive to courts in New York who are trying to resolve our client's issue. By using the *Katz* case, however, West can help us find other cases, which also discuss the implied obligation of good faith and fair dealing and which have been decided by courts in New York.[1] In this Chapter, we will be analyzing one of the cases that West will help you to find: *Geren v. Quantum Chemical Corporation.* Before reading the rest of this Chapter, please read the *Geren* case. Continue reading this Chapter after you have carefully read

---

1. Most cases involving large corporations or sovereigns that concern issues concerning bonds are filed in the federal courts in New York. Although the federal courts in New York will apply the law of the bond contract, which is usually New York law, their opinions are not binding on the state courts in New York. The highest authority on the law of New York is the Court of Appeals of New York.

the parts of the Geren Case that are relevant to your legal issue: Paragraphs [1], [2], and [3]. The text of the case now appears in your COURSE MATERIALS on your TWEN site.[2]

4.4.1 Evaluate a Case by Examining Its Citation

First, notice the text in the top left column of the case. This is called the Style of the case. The Style contains all of the information you need to evaluate the jurisdictional relevance of the case; it also contains the information from which the citation sentence that describes this case can be constructed. The citation sentence that describes this case begins with the names of the parties. These names are highlighted by Westlaw with all capital letters:

GEREN V. QUANTUM CHEMICAL CORPORATION[3]

Also in the upper left of the Westlaw case, you can see the parenthetical that tells you how to cite the case: (Cite as 832 F. Supp. 728).[4] The first few lines in the information at the upper left of the case show the court which issued the case: United States District Court for the Southern District of New York.[5] Finally, the date at the end of the Style tells you when the case was decided. It is customary to refer only to the year. The complete citation appears below.[6]

Geren v. Quantum Chemical Co., 832 F. Supp. 728 (S.D.N.Y 1993).

4.4.2 The West Summary

Just below the Style of the case, you will find the Summary paragraph prepared by West. It is not part of the actual case, so it is not part of the law. Reading through the summary, you can see that the case is about bonds and possible breaches of the bond agreement. You might be enticed to continue reading the materials supplied by West to see if you want to read this case.

4.4.3 West Headnotes

Just below the summary paragraph, you will find the West Headnotes. West provides these Headnotes to help you to evaluate the case. Each Headnote corresponds to numbered paragraphs in the opinion. For example, Headnote [1] has a title Corporations and a West Key Number 473. West divides the Corporations title into several subparts; the subpart numbered 101k473 concerns the contractual duty of good faith and fair dealing to bondholders by a corporation. West assigns this

2. You should have a copy of this case in front of you as you read the rest of this Chapter. You may either print the case or open it on your computer.

3. The Bluebook contains rules that allow you to abbreviate certain words. Corporation is one of those words. For a complete list, see Bluebook Table 6.

4. Again, the citation is based on the appearance of this case in a set of bound books called the Federal Supplement (F. Supp). This series of books contains all of the officially reported cases of the federal district courts.

5. See the Bluebook for a complete listing of the appropriate abbreviations for the U.S. District Courts.

6. See the back cover of the Bluebook for sample case name citations.

Headnote to a case if West believes that the case concerns this specific point of law. Of course, you must read the case yourself to determine whether the case is relevant to your legal problem. As you read the Headnotes, you can see that the beginning of the case appears to be about topics that are interesting to us. In fact, Headnotes [1], [2], and [3] all describe points of law related to our Urbania case. Notice, however, that the rest of the Headnotes discuss other issues, none of which seems relevant to our case. Often, a case will contain discussions of several issues, only some of which will be relevant to you. Reading efficiently, you should focus on only the parts of the case that directly affect your research.

Although Headnotes [1] and [3] seem to discuss relevant points, Headnote [2] seems to be the most relevant. In reading this opinion, you should read the beginning of the case so that you understand the factual background. You should focus on the paragraphs of the opinion that correspond to Headnotes [1], [2], and [3]. Because lawyers have so much to read, West has tried to help lawyers to efficiently choose which parts of opinions they might want to read. You can use the Headnotes to focus your reading of the cases that you find in your research.

Notice that the cases that you read in the textbooks for your other classes are usually not the full text of the opinions. The textbook editors choose only the relevant parts of the cases for the textbook. By providing the Headnotes, West allows you to create your own "textbook" versions of the cases that you find.

Before continuing this section of our text, please read (or re-read) the parts of the *Geren* opinion that correspond to Head-notes [1], [2], and [3]. Continue reading this text when you have finished. Also, open another window for the *Katz* case. We will be comparing the cases in the discussion that follows.

4.4.4   Evaluating a Court's Legal Argument

Now, let's focus on the relevant parts of the *Geren* case. Notice that Headnote [2] has the same title and Key Number as Headnote [8] of the *Katz* case. Each of these Headnotes is about Contracts. Specifically, each concerns the standard of law that courts will apply to decide whether a party has violated an implied obligation of good faith and fair dealing. West has assigned the Key Number 168 and the subpart 95k168 to these Headnotes. All cases that West has read that concern these subjects will be assigned this Headnote. In the *Katz* case, Headnote [8] contained the legal standard that the court in that case had articulated.

[8]   Contracts ☜168

95k168 Most Cited Cases

Where an implied contractual obligation to act in good faith and to deal fairly is asserted as basis for relief, it must be considered whether it was clear from what was expressly agreed upon that the parties who negotiated express terms of contract would have agreed to proscribe the acts later complained of as a breach of implied covenant of good faith had they thought to negotiate with respect to that matter.

In the *Geren* case, the legal standard is stated differently.

[2] Contracts ☞168

95k168 Most Cited Cases

Under New York law, every contract contains implied covenant of good faith and fair dealing to ensure that parties perform substantive terms of their agreements; however, implied covenant only imposes obligation consistent with other terms of contract.

Because this standard appears in a case decided by a federal court in New York that was applying New York law, you can infer that this is the standard used by New York courts. If you are reading the *Geren* case online, just click the [2] in the Headnote, and you will be taken to the part of the actual opinion that discusses this point of law. If you are reading a hard copy of the text, simply turn the pages until you find Paragraph [2] in the opinion.[7]

In this Paragraph [2], the court is going to discuss whether the facts of this case justify its finding that the defendants violated an implied covenant of good faith and fair dealing. This is extremely interesting to us because this is precisely the question that a court must address about Urbania. Pay careful attention to how the court discusses this topic and how it supports the legal conclusions that it reaches. As you read this section of the opinion, consider how a court might apply the same reasoning to the Urbania case. How are the facts of this case different? How would those facts possibly change the legal result?

4.4.5 Establishing the Prior Law: Step One in the CL Rubric

Notice that the court begins with a simple statement of the law. "Every contract governed by New York law, including the indenture at issue here [and the Urbania bonds], contains an implied covenant of good faith and fair dealing." *Geren v. Quantum Chemical Co.,* 832 F. Supp. 728, 731 (S.D.N.Y. 1993). The court then cites another federal district court case to support its proposition; however, the court wants to show that the federal court followed New York law, so it adds the information that the federal case cited a case from the New York Court of Appeals. The full citation appears below.

Hartford Fire Ins. Co. v. Federated Department Stores, Inc., 723 F.Supp. 976, 991 (S.D.N.Y.1989) (citing ***728** Rowe v. Great Atlantic & Pacific Tea Co.,* 46 N.Y.2d 62, 412 N.Y.S.2d 827, 830, 385 N.E.2d 566, 568–69 (1978))

---

7. Notice that you are on Page 3 of the Westlaw version of the case; however, the pagination is different in the original text. The numbers in bold face print refer to the pages in the original text. When you cite any case, you must cite to the page numbers in the original source.

The court expands on the general propositions of law that will govern its discussion to follow. The court relies on a mix of federal court cases and New York state cases. This opening paragraph gives the reader a framework to understand the next paragraphs where the court will analyze and compare similar cases. The cases cited establish some background legal principles. It is not necessary to explain the facts of these cases because they are being used to frame the discussion. The court is establishing that its opinion is based on the prior cases.

4.4.6 Explaining the Court's Rationale: Step Two in the CL Rubric

The remainder of Paragraph [2] displays the court's legal analysis. As you read this section, notice what the court is attempting to do. The judge must make a determination about whether the facts of the case before him constitute a violation of the implied covenant of good faith and fair dealing. There a number of ways that a judge might address that question. In the previous paragraph, the judge set out the legal principles that apply to this case. Because the implied covenant of good faith and fair dealing is a common law doctrine, the court must look to prior cases to find statements of the doctrine's basic principles. The various statements that the court cites comprise a statement of the law that seems quite similar to a code section you might find in a civil law system. Instead of referring to a code section as authority, however, the court must cite to prior common law precedent. That precedent will guide the judge's decision—just as a code section might guide the judge's decision in a civil law system.

To illustrate this, let's reformulate the sentences in the first paragraph of our Section [2] into the form of a code section:

New York Civil Code.

Section 111.10 **Implied Covenant of Good Faith and Fair Dealing**.

111.11 Every contract governed by New York law contains an implied covenant of good faith and fair dealing.

111.12 Such an implied covenant, however, can only impose an obligation consistent with other mutually agreed upon terms in the contract.

111.13 The covenant is violated when party to a contract acts in a manner that, although not expressly forbidden by any contractual provision, would expressly deprive the other of the right to receive the benefits under their agreement.

Compare this statutory formulation to the text in the *Geren* case. The main difference is that the formulation in the case cites other cases as authority. This common law doctrine exists only in the opinions of prior cases. Because this is a contract issue, it is a matter of state law. Courts must look to prior statements of law by the relevant courts. The judge in the *Geren* case looks to two types of courts—federal district court cases from the Second Circuit, which includes New York, and New York state courts. The federal court cases will be highly persuasive to the judge here, who is also a judge in a federal district court; however, this judge is aware that he must also cite precedent from the New York courts. All of this is similar to simply finding the right code provision. Instead of looking for the code section in a code book, our common law system requires us to watch the evolution of the law through the prior opinions. It is, however, no less "the law" than a code provision would be.

4.4.7 Comparing the Application of the Law in the Prior Case to the Present Case: Step Three in the CL Rubric

The "law" in the case is not simply the "rule" that you might be able to abstract from the case. The law of the case is that rule as it is applied to the facts of the specific case. Common Law Argumentation requires you to analyze each case as an individual application of legal principles to specific facts. Based on your analysis of how the courts of the relevant jurisdiction have decided the existing cases, you can predict how those courts might analyze the facts of your case. The rule alone is never enough; you must always be aware of how the courts have applied the rule to specific facts in specific cases.

Having set out the law by referring to prior precedents, the judge moves into the next phase of his analysis. In the same way that the judge finds the statement of the law in prior cases, he must also find the application of the law to the facts in those prior cases. The reasoning that the courts have used in prior interpretations of the law guides the judge in making a determination in the *Geren* case. In the following paragraphs, the judge shows how the other relevant courts have applied the law to other fact situations. This is an essential part of Common Law Argumentation. The statement of the legal principles is only the beginning. The court must also make a ruling that is consistent with the application of the law in other cases. This reference to precedent is just as much part of the law as the statement of the law itself. Without this part of the analysis, Common Law Argumentation is not complete.

First, the court discusses the *Van Gemert* case. *Van Gemert v. Boeing Co.*, 520 F.2d 1373 (2d Cir.), *cert. denied*, 423 U.S. 947 (1975). Notice the citation for this case. Because the case appears in the set of case reporters called the F. 2d, you know that the case is from a federal court of appeals. The notation in the parentheses after the citation—(2nd Cir.)—tells you that the case was decided by the Second Circuit, which includes New York. The notation, *cert. denied*, tells you that the case was appealed to the United States Supreme Court, but the Supreme Court denied the appeal to hear the case. The citation tells the reader that the case is a reliable source. Because a federal court may hear cases brought by parties of different states, it is not clear from the citation which state's law the court in *Van Gemert* is applying; however, because the Second Circuit deals mainly with New York law when it decides state law issues, a reader may infer that New York law is at issue here.[8]

In discussing the facts of *Van Gemert*, the court first gives the legally significant factual information from the case. The court must establish that this case is one where another court has applied the law of implied covenants of good faith and fair dealing to a factual situation that is similar in relevant ways to the case before it. The court is using this case as an example of a situation where a court has decided that an implied covenant of good faith and fair dealing has been violated. The court explains that the *Van Gemert* court was trying to decide whether a party to a contract violated an implied covenant related to an explicit notice provision in the contract. In its explanation of the case, the court first explains what the notice provision in the contract was intended to do—"allow [the bondholders] to determine whether they wanted to exercise the conversion privilege attached to their bonds." The court then explains the legally significant fact about this contract. Even though the contract contained a provision that required a notice to be given to the parties, it did not expressly specify the exact type of notice that was to be given; here the court is using Step 2 of the CL Rubric.

The question before the court was whether the type of notice that the parties received was sufficient under the contract. The court decided that it was not. Specifically, the court compared what it had determined to be the reason that the contract contained the notice provision in the first place—"allow [the bondholders] to determine whether they wanted to exercise the conversion privilege attached to their bonds"—to the actual notice given. The court determined that the notice given was inconsistent with the words of the contract.

Having given an example of how a party can violate an implied covenant of good faith and fair dealing, the court goes on to discuss a case where the covenant was not violated. Again, this application of the legal principles to a specific fact situation, which has already been decided by a relevant court, is part of the law in Common Law Argumentation. Judges follow the reasoning that prior judges have used so that the Common Law Argumentation can be consistent and predictable.

The *Geren* court next cites *Metropolitan Life Ins. Co. v. RJR Nabisco, Inc.*, 716 F.Supp. 1504, 1517 (S.D.N.Y.1989). The issue in *Geren* is whether it is a violation of an implied covenant of good faith and fair dealing for Quantum Chemical to incur debt to pay a special dividend. The bondholders allege that it is. The court begins its discussion of this case by noting that the facts of the case present an "almost identical legal issue to that presented here." The court then recounts the facts of the *RJR* case to highlight the similarity between those facts and the facts of the case in *Geren*. After setting out the facts, the court quotes the reasoning from the RJR opinion. By doing this, the court is signaling

---

8. It would be preferable for the court to have specified that. Recall that the Geren case itself discusses Virginia law later in the opinion. If the Geren case were to be cited on this point of Virginia law by another court, it is likely that the citation would contain a parenthetical explaining that the court was specifically applying Virginia law, even though it is a court in the Second Circuit.

that it will use this same reasoning to solve the *Geren* case. By reading
this quoted language, it is clear how the court is going to hold in the
case.

> There being no express covenant between the parties that would
> restrict the incurrence of new debt, and no perceived direction to
> that end from covenants that are express, this Court will not imply a
> covenant to prevent the recent LBO and thereby create an indenture
> term that ... was not bargained for here and was not even within
> the mutual contemplation of the parties.... These plaintiffs do not
> invoke an implied covenant of good faith to protect a legitimate,
> mutually contemplated benefit of the indentures; rather, they seek
> to have this Court create an additional benefit for which they did
> not bargain 716 F.Supp. at 1508, 1519.

A reader can see the parallels between the ruling in *RJR* and the
issue in *Geren*. The court immediately cites another case to support its
reasoning. This is another case where a judge found that a company that
engages in activities that are allowed by the terms of the bond contract
cannot be found to have violated an implied covenant of good faith and
fair dealing just because some of the bondholders are ultimately disad-
vantaged. Again, the court relies on the general prohibition that a court
cannot add new provisions to a contract. It seems to be adding another
rationale as well. The court's reasoning seems to imply that the parties
who are now complaining should bear the burden of insisting on contract
provisions that would protect them in cases where the borrower might
risk its financial stability. In essence, the court takes the view that it will
not add protections to a contract that the parties did not include
themselves. The court cites authority for this position, but it does not
give any of the facts of the cases. Each of the cases is from a New York
state court or from a federal court that has applied New York law.

The court adds a footnote citing an additional source for its opinion.
The American Bar Foundation is a professional lawyers group that
produces various guidelines for practitioners. Their documents have no
force of law; however, courts might cite them as additional support for a
legal argument. The case law that the court has cited provides the legal
basis for the courts opinion; the American Bar Foundation material is
simply additional support and is added in a footnote.

4.4.8 Making a Ruling: Step Four in the CL Rubric

Having laid a foundation in Paragraph [2] for its conclusions, the
court next applies the law to the facts before it in Paragraph [3]. The
court focuses on the facts of the case that it believes are legally
significant, based on its earlier discussion. First, the court mentions that
the contract does provide some restrictions on the company's ability to
take on additional indebtedness. The court points out, however, that
these restrictions do not specifically limit the amount of indebtedness
that the Company can incur. The court uses the law as announced in
prior cases to reach its conclusion for the case before it. The court relies

heavily on the *RJR Nabisco* case in its analysis. To complete its analysis, the court explains why the plaintiff bondholders have misunderstood the law of the *RJR Nabisco* case. Although the court concedes that there might be some factual differences between this case and the facts of *RJR Nabisco*, it concludes that "the issue in both cases is the same: whether such act violates implied covenants of the indenture." *Geren* at 733.

The court skips many steps in its legal reasoning, which readers must infer. In U.S. Legal Discourse, it is understood that courts must cite precedent and give a short explanation of their reasoning, but readers accept that the courts are decision-makers, and they are not required to give exhaustive explanations in their final opinions. One of the arts of Common Law Argumentation is to read court decisions and to infer what the court must have reasoned in order for it to make the decision that it gives. If a case involves a new point of law, a court may be more expansive in its explanation. For example, because the cases that come before the U.S. Supreme Court are generally new or difficult, the opinions sometimes contain more explanation than the opinions of other courts. Even so, U.S. Supreme Court opinions also leave much room for interpretation by later lawyers and judges.

Think about who is writing a legal opinion, like *Van Gemert*, and what his purpose is in writing it. First, it is written by a judge, who is required by law to decide the case in front of him. Under the U.S. Constitution, judges may only decide "cases in controversy," that is, judges do not give opinions on the law in the abstract. Their opinions are focused on the facts of the case before them. They do not need to describe the cases that they are relying on in any greater detail than necessary to decide the case before them. Often, you will see that a court has cited to another case on a point of law that is interesting to you. The court, however, will not say very much about what happened in the case. When that happens, you must find the case and read it yourself. In fact, one of the best ways to find cases that might be helpful to you is by reading the citations in cases that you find.

If you are writing a research memorandum to another lawyer, however, your purpose is quite different. Although you are ultimately going to decide the facts of the case before you (similar to the judge), your primary purpose is to explain the current law, which you are relying on, to the reader of your memorandum. It is that explanation that is the most important thing to your audience. It is often the reader (in your case, a Partner in the USLD Law Firm) who will make the final decision about how the law applies to the case. Your memorandum will help the Partner to decide. You must explain the current law so that the Partner has enough information to evaluate whether you are correct in your conclusion. A court can simply make a decision; it need not be overly detailed about its explanation. A lawyer must also make a decision; however, her explanation of the current law and how that law relates to the particular facts of the case she is addressing should be the focus of her memorandum. In the next Chapter, we will look carefully at

a legal memorandum and point out how it differs from an opinion of a
court.

4.5 CLOSE READING EXERCISE 4: EVALUATING AN ANALOGOUS CASE

As we have seen in this Chapter, courts refer to prior cases when
they decide new cases. When a court approaches a legal issue, it uses a
methodology similar to what we have been calling the CL Rubric. As you
become more familiar with United States Legal Discourse, you will begin
to use the CL Rubric to help you to recognize how other cases are
relevant to your legal research. For example, go to your COURSE
MATERIALS and read the case, *Metropolitan Life Ins. Co. v. RJR
Nabisco, Inc.* As you read the case, try to identify how the court has
constructed arguments based on its reading of prior cases. Further, try
to identify the specific parts of the opinion that are most relevant to the
legal issues in the Urbania case. Did the court in the *Van Gemert* case
use the *RJR Nabisco* case properly? What specific arguments could you
make about the Urbania case based on the reasoning in the *RJR Nabisco*
case?

Chapter 5

EVALUATING ANALYTICAL LEGAL WRITING: THE OFFICE MEMORANDUM

5.1 INTRODUCTION

One of the most common legal documents written by U.S. lawyers is the office memorandum. The primary purpose of the Office Memorandum is to provide the Partner who assigned the memorandum with the information needed to determine how to advise the client. Partners are always very busy people, with many cases to consider and many business lunches to attend. The Partner relies on the Associate to provide an analysis of the client's case, in the form of an Office Memorandum; this analysis relies on careful consideration of the legal theories that pertain to the client's case.

A central goal of the Office Memorandum is to explain the current law and to provide an analysis of how the law relates to the facts of the client's case. An effective Office Memorandum does not just provide undigested chunks of language from previous cases. Key to a memorandum being maximally useful for the Partner in making her decisions about how to advise the client is the thoughtful application of case law and Common Law Argumentation to the facts of the client's case. It is the Partner who must ultimately make the final decision about how to advise the client; this means that the Partner must ultimately decide how the law applies to the case. The Associate's memorandum is meant to provide crucial help that the Partner needs to make that decision.

Throughout this book we have noted that an excellent way to become familiar with conventions and preferred patterns of an unfamiliar discourse is close reading of successful documents valued by the discourse community, in our case the U.S. Legal Discourse Community. In this chapter, we will first discuss several key elements found in effective office memoranda. Then we will ask you to go to the TWEN site and read an example of an effective Office Memorandum that addresses the Urbania case. Accompanying the memorandum is extensive commentary which is meant to draw your attention to several aspects of the discourse—especially the Common Law Argumentation, the overall structure of the memorandum, and various language strategies that make the writing more accessible to the target audience. To appreciate why this memorandum is successful, the choices the writer made as he created the document, and the significance of the key elements of the memorandum, it is essential that you are aware of the audience and the needs of that audience. Thus, our first topic for discussion is the audience.

5.2 AUDIENCE FOR THE OFFICE MEMORANDUM

The primary audience for the Office Memorandum is the Partner, and possibly other Partners not familiar with the case. It is also possible that the client will read it. Thus the Associate must assume that not only readers who are knowledgeable about the facts of the case and some of the basics of the applicable laws, but also those who are potentially less familiar with both the facts and the case law. This means the Associate has a quite different audience to consider than the judge who writes the court's opinions. Consequently, the Associate often has to provide more complete summaries of prior cases and more explicit, full Common Law Argumentation in the Office Memorandum than is typically found in court cases.

All the members of this audience share some common goals and needs. They want to feel that they are using their time efficiently. Partners get rather grumpy if they feel they are squandering billable time making their way through rambling, not well analyzed legal documents. Of course, most important, the readers want a careful consideration of the applicable law and a well thought-out analysis of how the law applies to the facts of the client's case. They want to be assured that they can trust the analysis. The Associate can go a long way towards reassuring the reader of his reliability by meeting general expectations for a legal document. The readers also want to feel they get a maximum amount of information and insight about the case with a minimum amount of effort. One of the most important things a successful legal writer can do is to provide a document whose organization fits the arguments being presented. Another is to make the organization chosen highly salient to the readers. We will discuss how some of the introductory parts of the memorandum can provide this organizational framing which will make following the author's arguments easier for the reader. An effective U.S. legal writer pays attention to both content and form and how they successfully interconnect.

There is no single format for the Office Memorandum. In fact, each law firm will have its own preferred format. There are, however, some general aspects of organizational form that most law firms expect in Office Memorandum; they include a summary of the facts of the case, the Questions Presented and Brief Answers addressed in the memorandum, the Discussion in which the analysis of the existing law and how it applies to the case at hand appears, and the Conclusion. Before we turn to a discussion of each of these parts of the memorandum, it is important to consider how the legal writer can meet the readers' expectations.

5.3 MEETING THE EXPECTATIONS OF THE READER/THE WRITER'S PURPOSE

All readers, including Partners, come to a document with certain expectations about the form and general content of the document. If these expectations are not met, the reader gets confused or impatient or distrustful of the writer's analysis. Therefore, we begin by considering more fully the expectations of the readers of the Office Memorandum and how they connect to the writer's purpose.

First, the reader anticipates that the memorandum will introduce the client as well as the most salient facts of the case. In our current case, the reader needs to know that the Minister of Finance has met with the Partner and explained that his country is in danger of defaulting on bonds issued under New York contract law. The Minister has laid out a proposal to restructure Urbania's debt via a bond exchange. The proposal Urbania is considering involves use of a so-called exit amendment by which the bondholders who are willing to accept the new bonds will vote to delete the tax gross-up clause from the old bonds. The point of this maneuver is to lower the market value of the old bonds, thus encouraging the minority, who have not agreed to the exchange, to change their position.

Before Urbania proceeds any further with this exchange idea, it has asked your firm to write a legal opinion for them on some issues of law. The clients want to know whether the minority bondholders have legal grounds to challenge the proposed exit amendment. Specifically, the Urbanian Minister of Finance wants to know whether the exit amendment strategy, whose enactment would strip a negotiated bondholder protection from the existing bonds, violates any duties of good faith and fair dealing to bondholders. The introductory sections of the memorandum need to clearly articulate this information. It is true that the Partner has had the initial interview with the Minister of Finance and through that conversation been exposed to this basic information. However, some time may have lapsed between the initial interview and when the Partner reads the memorandum. In the mean time, the Partner is likely to have interviewed many other clients and to have been thinking about several other cases. A clear representation of the facts will help refresh the Partner's memory and get her ready to read the Associate's analysis. As we mentioned above, the memorandum is likely to have a broader audience than just the Partner, all of whom will expect and need a clear representation of the facts of the case. A well articulated summary of the facts will also reassure the client that the firm understands the client's perspective.

Finally, the memorandum provides part of an institutional record of the firm's dealing with the client; this record needs to be precise and complete.

In order for the Partner to offer the appropriate advice, she needs the Associate to write a memorandum explaining the likelihood that the minority bondholders can successfully challenge the exit amendment. She needs to know what legal theories minority bondholders have previously used to challenge similar actions by majority bondholders.

Because using exit consents in the sovereign context is a new idea, there may not be many cases involving sovereign governments, but such actions are likely to have been addressed within the corporate context. The Associate must be careful to look for cases beyond just those involving sovereign governments to cases involving New York contract law more generally. Two following questions are important for the Associate to address: 1) What legal arguments have been used in the corporate context to challenge similar actions by majority holders and corporate issuers? 2) Could those theories be used to block Urbania's proposed actions?

Just as authors of law review articles and judges have a point of view, authors of office memoranda have points of view. After all, when you give advice, you are taking a stand or offering an opinion of some sort. There will always be more than one way to relate the facts of the client's case to the existing law. There will be many potentially applicable laws. One of the purposes of the memorandum is to demonstrate how the law might fit in a new context, i.e. the particular context of the client's case. Often the particular facts of established cases will not provide a neat fit with the facts of the client's case. Then the writer must demonstrate how the same underlying legal principle is at issue in both cases. A major challenge is to create an argument that clearly shows how the case law that the writer has chosen fits with the facts of the client's case and provides a legal strategy for helping the client succeed.

Now go to the TWEN site and find the sample memo in the tab called Chapter 5: First Sample Memo with Suggested Comments. As you read the sample memo on the TWEN site, consider how the writer dealt with each of the issues raised above. How did the writer present the facts of the case? Did the writer include the client's motives and perspective? You will notice that the commentary that accompanies the memorandum addresses several issues concerning how the writer shaped the presentation of the facts. These comments are meant to raise your awareness of the writer's choices in presenting the client's case. As you read the memorandum, evaluate the legal approach the writer took towards the Urbania case. Are there other approaches you think might have been equally or perhaps even more effective? Can you identify specific writing strategies or arguments that allowed the writer to effectively meet the readers' expectations? Again, the commentary will help guide you in becoming more conscious of specific writing strategies and how they help meet the reader's expectations.

Now that you have a better understanding of the audience and its expectations, we turn to an overview of the memorandum. However, at this point we need to issue a caveat. Examination of examples of legal writing is meant to further your introduction to the U.S. Legal Discourse Community. Gaining an understanding of the kind of texts members of the U.S. Legal Discourse Community value can provide you with tools to help you as you read more about U.S. law and as you write various papers in your LL.M. career (and beyond). You should not take the examples we present as mandatory templates into which you should, or even could, fit your own arguments. Just as we cautioned you that you should not take the CL Rubric as an ordered, four-step template that should be slavishly adhered to, the exact form of an Office Memorandum will vary with the content being expressed. Keeping in mind that the exact form of office memorandum vary, let's consider the general organization of a typical memorandum.

5.4 THE OFFICE MEMORANDUM

5.4.1 Overall Organization of the Office Memorandum

The memorandum often begins with a short overview of the most salient facts of the case. The First Sample Memo that appears on the TWEN site begins with a brief introductory overview of the case. The overview acts as the initial framing for the memorandum. It provides the entree to the case and successful legal writers take care to use the introductory section to present the client's story in a way that is easy to for the reader to understand. It is important for the Partners to understand the client's perspective and motivation in order to determine if the strategy suggested by the firm will meet the client's goals. The client wants to feel that the firm has a personal stake in its well being, that it is being considered in a respectful way, not just as one more paying customer. The client's story is more than just a description of the facts of the case or a recounting of the chronological events that led the client to the law firm's door. Effective introductory sections include the relevant, key information about the problem the client is seeking to remedy and a succinct representation of any strategy the client might be proposing. (If an introduction is part of the memorandum, it is important to remember that a fuller version of the facts, with more specific detail will follow the introductory sections. That is the place for many of the specifics about, for instance, the exact terms of the bonds, such as the amount of the face value of the bonds; this level of detail will tend to bog down the initial introduction of the client's case.) Representation of the problem and the strategy for addressing the problem provides insight into the client's motivation in seeking the law firm's advice.

As you read the Introduction in the First Sample Memo on the TWEN site, consider how the writer dealt with each of the following issues: 1) What are the key pieces of information that the Partner needs in order to determine how to advise the client? A strategy for answering this question is to select the facts that are legally relevant. In other words, which facts raise issues that have been addressed previously by the U.S. legal system and will be addressed in the memorandum? Of course, the writer's understanding of what facts are legally relevant is filtered through and informed by reading of existing case law. 2) What are the motivations and reasoning the client has expressed that will help the Partner better understand its decisions and its goals?

The next section of the memorandum is a statement of the key Questions Presented that are raised by the client's case. The Questions Presented arise from the Associate's thoughtful analysis of applicable case law in relation to the facts in the client's case. The Questions Presented are followed by the Brief Answers.

After these introductory materials, which are meant to orient the reader to the overall picture, a fuller presentation of the facts typically follows. This fuller presentation provides the facts, including specific details relating to the two bonds, upon which the common law arguments will be build and assures the client that the firm is aware of all the pertinent facts. For instance, a fuller description of both the 2006 bonds and the 2018 bonds, with details about the interest rate and face value of the bonds is appropriate here. Also more details about the negotiations that have already taken place between the representatives of the Urbanian government and the bondholders, to provide a clearer picture of where agreement has been reached and where the sticking points are. This is a place for information about the motivation of Urbania and the majority bondholders to help the reader understand their reasoning—why the majority would agree to accept an exchange in which the face value of their bonds is actually lessened. A fuller explanation of just how the tax gross-up clause works and why its elimination would put pressure on the minority bondholders to agree to the exchange would be appropriate. After all, this is a relatively new strategy and all the Partners might not be aware of it.

The heart of the memorandum is a discussion of the relevant law that applies to these Questions Presented and the possible legal strategies growing out of the Associate's consideration of the relevant law. The goal is to advise the Partner on the likely outcome of pursuing the proposed legal strategies; this means it is important that the memorandum addresses possible problems with or counter arguments to the proposed strategies. Finally, the Associate concludes, by giving his or her best estimate as to the likely success of the proposed strategies.

Now that you have a general picture of how the Office Memorandum is structured and the purpose of each section, we turn our attention to the Questions Presented and their Brief Answers. As we will see, these sections of the memorandum introduce the reader to the legal issues the memorandum will focus on and so begin to articulate the Associate's Common Law Argumentation.

5.4.2   The Questions Presented and Brief Answers

Well crafted Questions Presented and their Brief Answers lay out the basic legal strategies that the Associate is suggesting the firm might follow as they go forward with the client's case. They serve as an abstract to the memorandum and thus provide the reader with a helpful orientation to the issues that will be raised in the body of the memorandum. Successful questions and answers also preview the overall organization of the discussion in the body of the memorandum, thus providing the reader with a useful roadmap of the arguments to be presented. They help set the reader's expectations about the information to be presented.

Below, are the Questions Presented and accompanying Brief Answers from the memorandum you will find on the TWEN site. We reproduce them here in order to facilitate a more in-depth discussion of how the Questions Presented work to both meet and set reader's expectations by providing a framework for the body of the memorandum. Consider the following questions:

Questions Presented

1. Under New York contract law, does Urbania, according to the amendment clause in the 2006 Bonds, need the consent of all bondholders in order to delete the tax gross-up clause?

2. Under New York contract law, would Urbania violate any duties of good faith and fair dealing if it deleted the tax gross-up clause in the 2006 Bond with the consent of the Majority Bondholders against the wishes of the Minority Bondholders?

Notice that both questions begin by clearly identifying the legal jurisdiction, New York state, and the type of law, contract law, that the writer will be addressing in the analysis of Urbania's legal situation. From our discussions in Chapters 3 and 4, you already know that jurisdictional issues are central to the U.S. legal system and so to U.S. Legal Discourse. The writer is fulfilling the expectations of the U.S. Legal Discourse Community, including the Partner(s), by paying close attention to the jurisdictional origin of the legal cases he will discuss in the memorandum. The 2006 Bonds were issued in New York, and they are covered by New York contract law. Therefore it is most appropriate that the Associate draws on New York law. Within the U.S. legal system, the precedents cited must be as persuasive as possible. Since the case will be controlled by New York law, New York law is most persuasive.

In Chapter 3, we noted that the argument presented in the law review article rested primarily on the *Katz* case, which was a Delaware case. If the writer of this memorandum tried to build the argument primarily on the *Katz* case, the argument would be on much weaker ground than by building the argument on New York law. By introducing the Questions Presented with reference to the legal jurisdiction of New York, the writer is signalling the Partner (and other readers) that he has found case law from the appropriate jurisdictional source. This tells the U.S. lawyer that the legal precedents that the Associate relies on to build his analysis will be given serious consideration by the Court. This builds the Partner's confidence in the Associate's analysis.

As you read the body of the memorandum, notice how the writer frames his arguments in terms of the jurisdiction in which the case was decided.

Consider why he is careful to point out how likely the court is to find an argument persuasive depending on which court decided the case. The majority of the cases that the Associate uses to build his case on are either New York state cases or cases from the 2nd Circuit within the federal court system, even though the fact patterns of these cases are quite different from the fact pattern of the Urbania case. Pay attention to how the *Katz* case is introduced and the care taken to discuss the probable persuasiveness of *Katz* with the New York Court. The writer notes that the fact pattern of the *Katz* case is actually much closer to the facts of the Urbania case than the New York cases he draws on. As you weigh the arguments, consider why the writer would choose to build the argument on cases whose fact patterns are quite different from those of the Urbania case.

The writer presents two questions: Question 1 asks whether unanimous agreement is required in order to delete the amendment clause in the 2006 bonds. This goes directly to the Urbania case and the proposed exit amendment strategy that the Finance Minister has asked the firm to investigate. It signals the reader that, by the writer's analysis, the answer to this question is foundational to the case. Moreover, the writer uses the language "according to the amendment clause in the 2006 Bonds." This signals the reader that the argument will likely focus on interpretation of the exact language of the bond. Question 2 narrows in on the issue of the duties of good faith and fair dealing that are considered part of any contract. Again, the question is framed in terms of the facts of the Urbania case.

The Questions Presented are followed by the Brief Answers. As you read through the memorandum, you will notice that the Brief Answers are organized with an initial YES/NO format, followed by a slightly expanded, one or two sentence answer. Often the slightly expanded answer is supplemented by specific subpoints. That is the case in the First Sample Memo.

The answers in this memorandum are particularly well crafted. They provide a solid overview of the legal issues that will be addressed in the Discussion section. Any reader who pays close attention to these answers will have a good idea of the main arguments and supporting reasoning that will appear in the body of the memorandum. Having such a well articulated preview of the argument helps the reader in a number of ways. For instance, it allows the reader to read with expectation about the arguments that will be made. It always easier to absorb and evaluate material that one is prepared for than new, unexpected material. The memorandum is supposed to be a maximally informative document, not a mystery novel. Having a clear preview also helps the reader understand the overall strategy the Associate is pursuing and the steps he is using to implement the strategy. All this helps the Partner to more easily follow and evaluate the quality of the analysis.

Now read the first part of the answer to Question 1 (*Under New York contract law, does Urbania, according to the amendment clause in the 2006 Bonds, need the consent of all bondholders in order to delete the tax gross-up clause?*):

1. Probably not. Based on the following reasons, the court would most likely find that Urbania has, according to the amendment clause, the right to delete the tax gross-up clause if it has the consent of the

> Majority Bondholders who hold more than 51% of the face value of the bonds:

Notice that the writer has answered the first question with a qualified "probably not". This immediately tells the reader that the Associate's general assessment is that the New York court will find that the language of the 2006 Bonds allows the tax gross-up clause to be deleted, if a majority of the bondholders agree to the action. The qualification "probably" tells the Partner that the Associate is not overstating the strength of the case. No one can be absolutely, 100% sure of what the court will decide. If the case were that straight forward and uncomplicated, the Urbanian Minister of Finance would not need your law firm's advice.

The answer is further elaborated by three subpoints which provide the basic points of the Associate's reasoning:

i) *It is reasonable to conclude that it would be in accordance with the language of the amendment clause because neither the face value nor the interests of the bond would be affected by the proposed amendment.*

ii) *It was the underlying purpose of the amendment clause and the intent of the parties to have the possibility to reschedule the bond structure in a practicable way without the bondholders' unanimous consent.*

ii) *The court would likely consider the Majority Bondholders' interest more important than that of the Minority Bondholders.*

The three subpoints tell the reader that the memorandum will provide three different arguments to support the writer's overall assessment concerning the court's likely ruling.

As you read through the subpoints, it is clear that the three arguments are distinct. The first addresses the language of the amendment, the second the notion of the contracting parties' underlying purpose for writing the amendment clause, and the third has to do with weighing the interests of the two contending parties in the case. A knowledgeable member of the U.S. Legal Discourse Community, such as the Partner, will take this as a signal that some New York cases exist that discuss each of these points.

Consider the first subpoint, pertaining to the significance of the exact language of the bonds. As you read through the Discussion, you will find that in the New York case, *Greenfield v Phillies Records,* the judge states that the intent of the parties who enter into a contract is best represented by the exact language of the contract. The writer also draws on a federal case from the 2nd Circuit, *Sharon Steel v Chase Manhattan,* in which the court emphasizes narrow interpretation of the language of the contract.

Notice in the first subpoint that the writer specifically mentions the face value of the bonds and the interest on the bonds; these are key provisions that are explicitly protected by unanimous agreement in the amendment clause of the 2006 Bonds. We see that even in the incipient formation of the argument the writer is bringing together prior case law and the particular facts of the case at hand. This reflects Common Law Argumentation, or thinking like a U.S. lawyer. As you consider the other subpoints of the Questions Presented, see if you can identify similar patterns of common law thinking.

5.4.3 Interconnection Between the Questions and the Discussion Section: Signaling the Organization of the Discussion

A well crafted set of Questions Presented and Brief Answers not only provides the reader an overview of the argument to be presented, they can also serve as an outline to alert the reader to the organization of the argument. The organization is also signalled by bolded headings throughout the Discussion section. Clear, bolded headings act as road map for reader as they are reading the document. They also let the busy Partner quickly go to specific sections she is particularly interested in.

As you read through the Discussion section, you will see that the writer divides the discussion with three main headings:

A. *Urbania would not be immune from the courts in the United States of America and the same law applies as to private citizens.*

B. *It would be in accordance with the amendment clause in the 2006 Bonds if Urbania deleted the tax gross-up clause.*

C. *Urbania would not breach the duty of good faith and fair dealing if it deleted the tax gross-up clause.*

You may be surprised by the first bolded heading. It does not relate to the Questions Presented and Brief Answers and so is unexpected. Section A lays out the case law that establishes that, for the purposes of commercial activities, such as issuing bonds and entering into other contracts, sovereign nations are treated like any other commercial agent. Being a sovereign nation does not exempt Urbania from U.S. law. The writer's decision not to include this issue in the Questions Presented and Brief Answers represents a deliberate, writerly choice that has an effect on the reader. It signals that the writer believes this principle is so well established that it should not be treated as a central legal question in the firm's analysis of the Urbania case. Nevertheless, it is a sufficiently significant point that the Associate wants to address it and "put it to rest" before proceeding to the substantive points that are at issue in the case. However, by not mentioning the issue in the Questions Presented and Brief Answers, the writer runs the risk of confusing the reader. The Questions and Brief Answers set the readers' expectations for what will follow. Following Question 1, the reader is set for a discussion of the language of the bond. Although a knowledgeable reader, like the Partner, will most likely quickly understand the purpose of this first section, her task will be made somewhat more difficult without a signpost alerting her that this will be the first legal issue presented.

Notice that the heading for section B (*It would be in accordance with the amendment clause in the 2006 Bonds if Urbania deleted the tax gross-up clause*) is a direct answer to Question 1 (*Under New York contract law, does Urbania, according to the amendment clause in the 2006 Bonds, need the consent of all bondholders in order to delete the tax gross-up clause?*). The heading for section C (*Urbania would not breach the duty of good faith and fair dealing if it deleted the tax gross-up clause*) is a direct answer to Question 2 (*Under New York contract law, would Urbania violate any duties of good faith and fair dealing if it deleted the tax gross-up clause in the 2006 Bond with the consent of the Majority Bondholders against the wishes of the Minority Bondholders?).* In these cases, the Questions Presented do act as clear sign posts for the reader.

Within section B, it is possible to map out the argumentation according the three subpoints provided in Brief Answer 1. The answer to Question 2 is more complex, as signalled by the fact that it has five subpoints. In studying the memorandum on the TWEN site, you may find it useful to map the subpoints provided in Question 2 to the actual discussion.

The memorandum on the TWEN site has a second brief answer. As you read it, ask yourself the following questions. Why does the writer hedge the answer, rather than straightforwardly answering YES or NO? What are the main points of law the writer will be developing to support his opinion that the court will probably decide that deleting the tax gross-up clause does not violate any duties of good faith and fair dealing? The writer lists five subpoints to this answer. This immediately tells the reader that the answer to this question will be rather complex. With complex arguments, the reader should expect the reasoning to be cumulative, with references back to earlier points. (Notice that point number v), the final argument, references both the U.S. District Court and the Court of Chancery of Delaware. The commentary on the side of the memo will help with this as it directs your attention to many of the important aspects of the Questions Presented and Brief Answers. It is meant to support and guide your analysis of each section of the memorandum and to raise your awareness of how the memo is crafted.

We have noted that the Questions Presented and Brief Answers are framed in terms to the prior case law as it applies to the client's case. Thus, they are framed from a common law perspective. In the next section we revisit Common Law Argumentation and the CL Rubric in more detail.

5.4.4   The Discussion Section: Common Law Argumentation, Again

Consideration of prior case law and how the fact patterns of the clients' case compare to those of appropriate case law will make up the bulk of any memorandum. Common Law Argumentation is essential to a successful memorandum. The the common law analysis is in fact the heart of the case. Therefore this is a useful point at which to remind ourselves one more time of the nature of Common Law Argumentation by reviewing the Common Law Rubric. The commentary which accompanies the First Sample Memo on the TWEN site provides an analysis of the points the writer is making. Rather than recapitulating the arguments made in the sample Memo, this section will focus on a few examples of Common Law Argumentation taken from other memoranda.

The overall issues of U.S. legal thinking we address here are parallel to the issues addressed in the First Sample Memo on the TWEN site. Keeping the CL Rubric in mind and actively attending to the Common Law Argumentation found in the memorandum should deepen your understanding of a legal argument that successfully meets the expectations and needs of the U.S. legal audience.

Recall there are typically four aspects to a full Common Law Argument:

1) Identification of a legally significant prior case and the key, legally significant facts of that case

2) Explanation of the rationale the court used in deciding the case

3) Explanation of how the facts in the prior case are either similar to or different from the facts of the client's case

4) An explanation of how the court **is likely** to rule on the client's case.

Keeping the CL Rubric in mind, consider the following answer to the question, which turns out to be important for the Urbania case: Does a sovereign nation have the same legal status as a corporation?

ANSWER 1

A sovereign state is a "political community whose members are bound together by a tie of common subjection to some central authority, whose commands those members must obey," Black's Law Dictionary 665 (2nd pocket ed. 2001). A corporation is an "entity (usually a business) having authority under law to act as a single person distinct from the shareholders who own it and having rights to issue stock and exist indefinitely" Black's Law Dictionary 147 (2nd pocket ed. 2001).

These definitions show some of the evident differences between sovereign states and corporations. For instance, considering their nature, a sovereign state is a political entity and exists under international law; corporations are not political entities, but rather business entities, that exist primarily under national laws. While a sovereign state has a direct and strong relationship to a specific territory and group of people, corporations are normally related to a group of share holders but their relation with a territory is not so important. Considering their commitments, sovereign states have social, political and economic duties to their citizens; corporations have principally economic duties to their stock and shareholders. Because the entities are so different in their natures and duties, it is not logical that they should have the same legal status in cases brought before a court.

If you're scratching your head and searching in vain for the elements of the CL Rubric, your thinking is on the right track. This argument is based on an appeal to authority, in the form of definitions from a well known legal dictionary, and a certain logical appeal. In many ways nations and corporations do seem to have quite different characteristics and so would logically not have the same status. However, this argument is not based on any case law. It would fail to convince U.S. lawyers.

Now let's consider a second answer to the question:

*The court **would likely** treat the sovereign nation, Urbania, under the same laws as a corporation.*

The New York District court has admitted litigation against sovereign states in their commercial activities and has established that the same law that is applied to private citizens in this kind of activity governs a sovereign nation's commercial actions.

The main statute addressing this point is the Foreign Sovereign Immunities Act of 1976 (FSIA) which gives District Courts original jurisdiction in actions against foreign states in those cases where sovereignties developed commercial activities. § 28 U.S.C.A. 1130(a), 28 1602 et seq, 1605 (a) (1). Even though the statute does not define commercial activity, there is a case which bears on this issue.

In Republic of Argentina and Banco Central de la Republica Argentina v. Weltover Inc., 504 U.S. 607, 112 S. Ct. 2160 (1992), Argentina, a sovereign nation, issued bonds and negotiated them on the international market as a way of refinancing its sovereign debt. The Supreme Court of the United States, looking at the nature of the activities, ruled that these actions were commercial transactions that should be governed by contract law. In other words, the Court held that commercial activities of this sovereign nation should be governed by the same law as private and corporate commercial activities.

*The facts of the Argentina v Weltover case are very similar to our client's situation. Urbania is a sovereign nation; it is issuing bonds that are going to be negotiated on the international market and the reason for doing so is to refinance its sovereign debt. Since prior case law establishes that a sovereign nation engaged in a commercial activity, such as issuing bonds, is acting in the manner of a private individual or corporation and can be treated as such, **it is reasonable to conclude** that the Court **is very likely** to determine that our client is involved in a commercial activity and that these activities **should be** governed by contract law.*

The first sentence in this answer represents Step 4 in the CL Rubric, the author's prediction as to how the Court is likely to rule. Notice that the writer hedges her opinion with the language *would likely*; this is appropriate because the lawyer cannot know with 100 percent certainty how the judge will rule on a case. The second sentence provides a general overview of how the Court has ruled on this issue in the past.

The next sentence represents Step 1 in the CL Rubric. It provides specific information about a pertinent statute, FSIA. Then the author provides a transition between the information about the applicable statute and a prior case that addresses the issue.

The fourth paragraph represents Steps 1 and 2 in the CL Rubric. The first sentence gives us the basic, relevant facts of *Argentina v*

Weltover, that Argentina issued bonds in order to refinance its sovereign debt. The second provides the Court's rationale for determining that these activities should be governed by contract law.

The fifth paragraph begins with Step 3 in the CL Rubric. The author explicitly compares the fact pattern found in *Argentina v Weltover* and the Urbania case. In both cases, sovereign nations are involved in issuing bonds in order to refinance their sovereign debt. The final sentence represents Step 4; it provides the writer's prediction that the Court is likely to conclude that since Urbania is engaging in commercial activity in the restructuring of its debt, its actions should be governed by contract law. Again note the bolded phrases that indicate the writer's appropriate hedges.

As you read the First Sample Memo on the TWEN site, you should be particularly alert for Common Law Argumentation. The commentary on the side of the memo will help with this as it directs your attention to Common Law Argumentation, including the various steps identified in the CL Rubric.

5.4.5 The Conclusion

Legal memoranda usually end with a separate Conclusion section. The Conclusion tends to be short, only one or two paragraphs. It provides the Associate's overall assessment of how the law applies to the case. In writing a conclusion, it is important to remember that the firm is paying the Associate to provide analysis, not to write an encyclopedia article. Even though the Partner will ultimately be the one who decides which legal approach to take, Partners value creative, thoughtful applications of the law. They want a reasoned, appropriately nuanced prediction on how the court is likely to rule, given the prior case law. A successful conclusion provides this. In a well crafted memorandum, the conclusion echoes the questions posed at the beginning and then provides short answers that are well supported in the body of the memorandum. Any reader should be able to read the introductory material and then go to the conclusion and get a good overview of the basic facts of the case, the issues it raises in relation to prior case law, and the writer's best estimation of how the court is likely to find and why. Often the conclusion will include brief allusion to the rulings provided by prior case law that the writer is relying on. However, details concerning exactly which cases are being referenced are not necessary here. They are provided in abundance in the Discussion section.

5.5 CLOSE READING EXERCISE 5: ANALYZING AN OFFICE MEMORANDUM

Now go to the TWEN site and click on the tab called Chapter 5: Close Reading Exercise 1 with Suggested Comments. As we have noted, you will also find extensive accompanying commentary on the side of this text. The commentary models the kinds of observations a reader makes when she is performing a 'close reading' of a document. It is meant to provide you with a kind of guided tour of the multiple facets that make up a successful legal memorandum. As we have noted throughout this chapter, the commentary will point out many instances of Common Law Argumentation, decisions the writer has made concerning the organization of the document, and writerly strategies the author has employed to make the information more precise and more accessible for the reader. You will also find commentary concerning audience expectation and how the writer attempts to meet that expectation.

You may want to read the First Sample Memo through once without referring too much to the commentary. As you do this initial reading, you should actively ask yourself questions about how the writer sets your expectations of how the arguments will be presented; what kind of cases the writer chose to base his analysis on; how he attempted to apply prior court decisions to the new context of the Urbania facts, etc. After you have read the memorandum and considered these issues on your own, return to the memorandum and re-read it also considering the commentary. You may be surprised at how many aspects of writing you were unaware of even as you read carefully and thoughtfully. Reading the memorandum to better understand the facts, applicable law, and effective analysis is one half of close reading of the text; the other half is paying attention to the ways in which the writer crafted the text and the choices the writer made in order to create a text that effectively connects with a U.S. legal audience. Remember, to learn the discourse conventions of an effective Office Memorandum, you should read for both content and form.

†